Trees of Algonquin Provincial Park

1996

First Printed 1987,
Revised and Reprinted 1989, 1993 and 1996

By Dan Strickland

With the **technical advice and assistance** of Alan G. Gordon
and Jack Mihell and the following other employees of, or
consultants to, the Ontario Ministry of Natural Resources and
the Algonquin Forestry Authority: Harvey W. Anderson,
Kenneth A. Armson, I.D. (Joe) Bird, Bill Brown, Daniel F. Brunton,
Donald F. George, C. Grant Head, M.M. (Mack) McLean,
Bob McRae, Ron Pittaway, Ron Tozer, Mike Turner, and
Dave Wray.

Photographs by John Hickie (77), Michael Runtz (38),
Mary I. Moore (17), Alan G. Gordon (12), Dan Strickland (9),
Algonquin Park Museum (8), Harry A. Thomson (6),
Communications Services Branch MNR (2), Jack Mihell (2),
Ontario Tree Seed Plant (2), Nancy Checko (1),
William J. Crins (1), Marc Denis (1), Steve Desjardins (1),
William Reynolds (1), Peter Smith (1).

Diagrams by Scott Down

Printed on
recycled paper

Published by:

The Friends of
Algonquin Park
P.O. Box 248
Whitney, Ontario
K0J 2M0

In Cooperation with:

Ministry of
Natural
Resources

Ontario

Cover Photo: Named for a former Park naturalist who intervened to save it from a
highway widening program, the Grant Tayler White Pine was a familiar landmark to
hundreds of thousands of visitors to Algonquin Park. The tree fell in a violent
windstorm Friday, November 13, 1992. *(Cover Photograph by Dan Strickland)*

Dan Strickland

Hardwood (deciduous) forest typical of Algonquin's west side

White Pine forest characteristic of east side

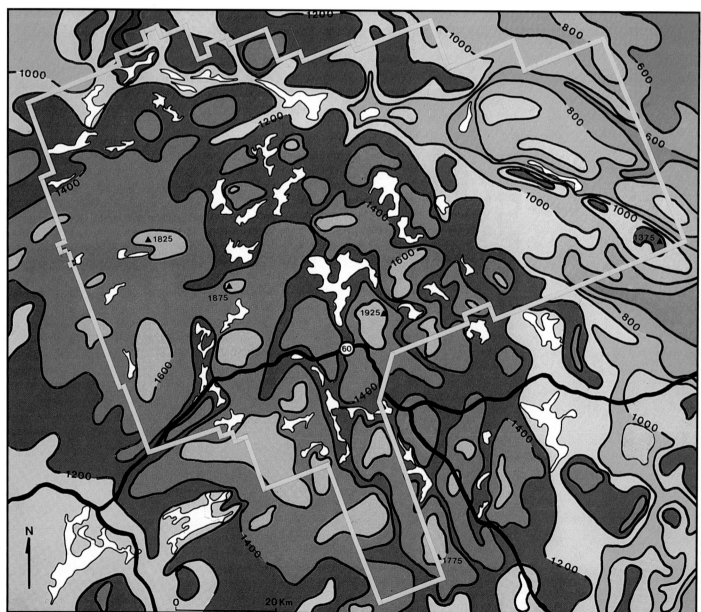

2 **The high elevations (shades of brown) of Algonquin's western two thirds have soils mostly derived from ice-deposited till and support hardwood forests. The low elevations (shades of green) on the Park's east side have large areas of sandy outwash plains that support pine**

The Trees of Algonquin Provincial Park

Of all the living things that inhabit Algonquin Park, none are more important than trees. The trees are far and away the largest organisms we have here; they almost completely blanket the landscape; they have an overwhelming influence in the lives of wildlife and smaller plants; they have been the backbone of the Park region's economy for a century and a half; they supply our modern society with large volumes of valuable wood; and, in form and colour, they are often profoundly pleasing to the human eye.

Yet, in spite of all this, the trees of Algonquin are very often taken for granted. Except at the peak of fall colours, many people pay hardly any real attention to our trees and often leave the Park unaware of just how interesting they actually are.

It is our hope in this book to help correct this tendency by relating some of the intriguing stories about the trees of Algonquin. We will first describe how individual tree species are distributed in the Park—they are by no means all mixed in together—and how this distribution subtly reflects the small but very real differences of climate and soil that occur across the great breadth of Algonquin. We will then look at each kind of tree in more detail, particularly with regard to how each succeeds in the struggle to survive and how each influences the lives of other plants and animals. Finally, we will examine the economic importance of the Park's trees and look at the scientific principles by which they are now managed.

Throughout the book we will attempt to draw your attention to some of the overlooked beauties of trees—for example, the crimson flowers of Red Maple, the purple and yellow flowers of spruce, and the pastel spring colours put on each year by the forests of Algonquin.

Although the book is not intended primarily as a field guide, the photographs should enable you to identify virtually any Park tree you encounter. Using our arbitrary dividing line between small trees and large shrubs—we have chosen not to include any willows or mountain ashes, for example—the Park has only 34 kinds of native trees and eight of these have very limited distributions, leaving only 26 really common species within our boundaries. With a little practice you can quickly become adept at identifying all Algonquin's trees, even from a distance, and this will open the door to a fascinating new dimension to your enjoyment of the living world that is Algonquin Park.

Algonquin Forests — A Subtly Controlled Mosaic

Most visitors to Algonquin know only the Corridor along Highway 60 or perhaps those parts accessible by canoe north or south of the highway. Collectively, this area is known as the "west side" of the Park and it typically has rounded hills covered with forests of deciduous, broad-leaved trees, mostly Sugar Maple, while, in the low areas between the hills and along lakeshores, the tree cover consists of conifers—spruce and fir, cedar and hemlock. This picture repeats itself again and again, mile after mile, so that many visitors may understandably assume that all of Algonquin's forests follow the same pattern.

In fact, the eastern third of the Park has distinctly different forests. Broad, level areas support stands heavily dominated by aspen or pine, usually White Pine or Red Pine but in some cases Jack Pine. Ridgetops, if they don't also have pine, very often are dominated by rather scrubby Red Oak. In either case, the forests of Sugar Maple so characteristic of the Park's west side are noticeably less common and the east side has an entirely different feel to it.

The reason for these striking differences between east and west side forests basically lies with an event that took place 500 million years ago. A period of violent mountain building occurred in what is now the west side of Algonquin Park and, although the mountains are now mostly eroded away, enough of their roots remain so that west side elevations are significantly higher than those of surrounding areas. For example, many hilltops in the Hwy 60 area reach well over 500 metres above sea level whereas, on the Park's eastern boundary, the land dips to a mere 170 metres above sea level.

This elevational difference has three important consequences

as far as Park forests are concerned. First, because it is higher, the west side is cooler than the east side. On average, the west side has about 84 frost free days every year whereas the east side gets 105. Second, because our weather systems generally move from west to east, the high elevations on the Park's west side force air masses entering the Park to rise, to cool, and very often, to lose more of the moisture they contain (as rain or snow) than they otherwise would have. Conversely, it tends to rain and snow less on the east side, not only because it is lower and warmer there, but also because much of the moisture in the easterly flowing weather systems has already been lost in the highlands to the west. We normally associate this sort of "rain shadow" phenomenon with truly mountainous areas but even the relatively slight elevational rise of the "Algonquin dome" has measurable effects. The west side receives 100 cm of precipitation annually (33% as snow) and the east side receives 90 cm (26% as snow).

The third and most important consequence of the east-west altitude difference has to do with the soils in the two areas. All of Algonquin Park was covered by huge ice sheets four or perhaps more times in the last one million years and the last glacier receded from the Park area just 11,000 years ago. The ice removed some previously existing soil but also deposited the forerunner of what we have today. On the Park's high, west side the ice left a layer up to 50 cm thick of variously ground up material that had been pushed along under the ice and then another coarser, more "gravelly" layer of material that had actually been inside the ice and which was dumped on the ground when the glacier finally melted. Collectively, these two layers are called till and they are now the base for most soils on the Park's west side.

The same process basically happened on the east side also but then something else occurred as well. As the great continental glacier retreated northwards, the basins of present day Lakes Huron and Michigan to the west of the Park's western highlands were filled by a huge body of glacial meltwater called Lake Algonquin. For a while the great lake drained to the south through what is now the Mississippi Valley but then, as the ice which fed the lake melted farther north it uncovered a lower outlet—to the east this time—at a place called Fossmill just outside the Park's northern boundary. An immense new river was born running across the northern and eastern parts of the Park area to the Ottawa Valley. Its currents carried staggering quantities of sand and other fine debris and where the river widened, great sand beds were deposited. Eventually, even lower outlets for Lake Algonquin were exposed and the Fossmill drainage ceased to operate but the broad, sandy "outwash plains" it created are still there, covering large areas of Algonquin's east side. The coarse structure of these water-deposited soils (and often their considerable depth) means that they retain moisture much less effectively than the ice-deposited tills on the Park's west side. This soil difference accounts for most of the remarkable change observed in Algonquin's forests as you travel from one side of the Park to the other.

It is also true, however, that very striking differences in forest type can occur in very small areas. In fact, the juxtaposition of radically different forest types is a well-known characteristic of Algonquin Park, particularly on the west side. There, it is quite literally possible, for example, to be looking one moment into a bog covered with Black Spruce (just as you could hundreds of kilometres to the north) and then, merely by turning around, to be looking up a hill into a hardwood forest of Beech and Sugar Maple (just as you could in extreme southern Ontario). Such "night and day" differences are accounted for mainly by the slightly cooler climate and the year-round wetness of the lowland sites, caused by the water percolating downwards through the thin soil overlying the bedrock cores of the hills. And, even within supposedly uniform forest types, different tree species tend to sort themselves out according to subtle but recognizable patterns. In hardwood forests, for example, Sugar Maple may be found throughout but Beech tends to be on the better drained hilltops and Yellow Birch is more prominent on the middle or lower slopes where the soil is slightly damper.

All of these nuances, however, are expressions of a single, basic truth about trees—and all living things for that matter. None of them just "happens to be there". Trees struggle against great odds and hazards for a place in the sun and each is subtly equipped to do better than its competitors in certain precise conditions. When conditions change, so too will the species

Michael Runtz

Aerial view of the old pine in the Big Crow nature reserve

The base of a giant

Algonquin Park Museum

A lone survivor from pioneer logging days

Male flowers

John Hickie

White Pine foliage

An old cone

Michael Runtz

On the shore of Tea Lake

4

most likely to be victorious. That is why the mosaic of forest types covering Algonquin Park is no accident but a sensitive indication of the underlying conditions of soil type, moisture, climate, and stand history. And because forest types control the lives of all the smaller plants and all the animals that live in them, these differences are of much more than passing interest.

Algonquin Park's Native Tree Species

The following accounts describe Algonquin Park's 34 native species of trees. There are ten conifers or "softwoods" (including three pines, three spruces, a cedar, a hemlock, a fir, and a larch). They all produce seeds in woody cones and have narrow, often needle-like leaves. With the exception of Tamarack (our one larch), they keep much of their foliage all year long.

The other 24 Algonquin trees are deciduous species (also known as hardwoods) belonging to eight separate families but nevertheless sharing some common characteristics. Their seeds are produced in a fundamentally different way from that of the conifers, the leaves are soft, broad and flat, and, of course, the leaves are shed each fall.

The Conifers

White Pine
Pinus strobus
Pin Blanc

The White Pine is Algonquin Park's tallest tree, its most important tree—at least historically—and, in the opinion of many people, its most beautiful tree. Indeed, these considerations apply to Ontario as a whole—which is why the White Pine was chosen as the province's official tree in 1984.

Its soft clear wood and tremendous size established its value very early on in our history as ideal raw material for products ranging from furniture right up to ship masts for the British navy. The fact, too, that felled trees could be floated down wild rivers to the Ottawa and St. Lawrence and thence shipped to market made it practical to exploit tremendous forests of White Pine over vast, roadless areas of eastern Canada, including what is now Algonquin Park. Since the story of the colourful early White Pine trade is told in many other places (including the Algonquin Logging Museum near the Park's East Gate and in *A Pictorial History of Algonquin Provincial Park*, another book in the same series as this one) we will not repeat the details here. It should never be lost from sight, however, that this early industry had a tremendous impact on the history of our country and on its forests.

Today, White Pine is still an important part of the Algonquin Park forests, especially on the east side. There, areas that were "solid pine" back in the 1830s when the first pioneer loggers pushed up the Petawawa and Barron rivers are still solid pine today. The somewhat warmer and drier climate of the east side and especially its sandier soils, left by glacial meltwater 11,000 years ago, all help make that part of the Park ideal for pine. Almost none of the trees there are surviving giants from the days before logging (and the attendant greater frequency of destructive forest fires) but some of today's new generation of east side pine are reaching fair sizes. The trees behind the Achray campground on Grand Lake, for example, are about 100 years old and 25 metres high.

On the west side of Algonquin Park, White Pine today is common enough but is mostly associated with rocky lakeshores and islands, exposed cliff tops and other oddball places—even bogs at times—where there is sufficient light and lack of competition from other trees to allow the pines to get established. White Pine is rather scarce, however, in the principal forests of the west side—the hardwood forests of Sugar Maple, Beech and Yellow Birch that cover most upland areas. Originally, they were much more common in the hardwoods than they are today—sometimes as stands or groves but also, and perhaps more usually, as scattered trees that towered above the surrounding broad-leaved species. Logging, and in some cases subsequent fire, in the 1800s and early years of this century removed almost all of this White Pine element and severely reduced the ability of the species to replace itself in the west side hardwoods. Today, there are only two places, in fact, where good examples of the "old-growth" White Pine-hardwood

association remain—at Dividing Lake just outside the Park's southwest boundary and in a nature reserve zone near the Crow River in the centre of Algonquin. Here, modern canoeists can hike a two km trail south from the river to marvel at a few of the magnificent old pine, many of them 40 metres (130 ft.) or more in height. You should take advantage of this opportunity while it lasts. Many of these trees have started to die and we expect that most will be gone in the next few decades.

Although the west side soils, derived from glacial till, are capable of growing the Park's biggest and best White Pine, the only remaining examples are over 300 years old and when they die they are not likely to be replaced. It is an amazing fact that such a mighty organism, weighing perhaps 60 tonnes or more, begins life as a tiny seed (of which it takes about 60,000 to make a kilogram) and success for a White Pine seed is anything but assured. To get started, for example, a White Pine seed must usually land on pine litter or, better still, on fresh, exposed mineral soil, but everywhere you look in a hardwood forest you see a thick layer of matted, dead, deciduous leaves. And, even if a pine seedling does get established, it must receive a lot of sunlight—not necessarily full sunlight but at least 45% of the full amount if it is to sustain the maximum potential growth and be a contender in the competition with other young trees. Once again, a typical, west side hardwood forest falls far short of providing the necessary conditions for the growth of new White Pine.

Pine needles grow in bundles of five (White Pine) or two for all other species found in the Park. From left the right: Scot's Pine (not native but planted in many places along Highway 60), Red Pine, White Pine, and Jack Pine.

How then, did the original big White Pine get established 300 years ago? This question is especially interesting because we know from examining ancient pollen preserved in bogs and lake bottom sediments that the forests of Algonquin have been essentially the same for the last 5000 years. In other words, the big White Pine somehow managed to get established in a hardwood forest—they were not lingering remnants of an earlier pine forest. Most authorities believe that the White Pine owed their beginnings to a series of ground fires that swept through the hardwoods, perhaps in some unusually warm and dry fall weather. Such fires would kill maple seedlings, destroy the leaf litter, dry out the forest floor, and expose the mineral soil—all of

John Hickie

Jack Pine on Carcajou Bay

Female flower

John Hickie

Male flowers and cone

John Hickie

Old but unopened cones

Fire opens cones

Michael Runtz

Red Pine bark

Male flowers

John Hickie

Michael Runtz

Cone developing

Mary I. Moore

Mature cone

Red Pine with typical, coarse, clustered foliage

6

which would favour pine seedlings. At the same time, the fire would kill enough of the overhead trees that the pine seedlings received enough light to make a go of it. It seems a slender set of circumstances but we know something along these lines must have occurred and, of course, it would only have to happen once every three or four hundred years for the White Pine component of the west side hardwoods to be perpetuated.

At the present time, the seed source for any potential White Pine comeback has been greatly reduced, or eliminated altogether in some areas, and, even more important, we humans presently make a practice of putting out the forest fires that might prepare a seedbed for new White Pine seedlings. It could even be speculated that lightning-induced fires are less likely in today's pineless hardwoods than they were in the old days because, then, lightning would have struck the tall, flammable pine rather than the lower, inflammable hardwoods as it does now!

For all these reasons, not to mention the tremendously long time it takes to grow really large pine, we are not likely to see a return to the conditions of 150 years ago when big pine dominated just about all of the Algonquin landscape. We will have to settle for the present reality in which White Pine dominates the east side and has a more modest role in the west.

Jack Pine
Pinus banksiana
Pin gris

Jack Pine lacks the impressive size and grace of Algonquin's other two pines and, for a novice in tree identification, might not be recognized as a pine at all. It rarely exceeds 15 metres in height or achieves a trunk diameter greater than 25 cm and, especially in open situations, often has a sprawling, untidy appearance. The bark, which is dark and flaky, and the needles, which are borne in clusters of two like the Red Pine but are much shorter, also help make the Jack Pine look very different from the other two species. Still, in its own way, Jack Pine does have a rugged, contorted beauty of its own. Indeed, one Algonquin Jack Pine on the shore of Grand Lake south of Achray was the subject of one of Canada's most famous landscapes, Tom Thomson's *Jack Pine*, painted in 1916.

Even more than the White Pine and the Red Pine, Jack Pine is predominantly a tree of the east side. As a matter of fact, only three Jack Pine trees can be seen along the entire length of the Highway 60 Parkway. Two trees are 60 m across a small pond on the north side of the highway 1 km outside the East Gate, and the other is directly opposite the road leading to Cache Lake. On the east side, however, Jack Pine is not only common, it is the dominant tree in many places. Once again, the warmer and drier conditions encountered in the low areas of Algonquin's east side seem to make a tremendous difference—in this case the difference between virtual absence and great abundance of Jack Pine. The greater prevalence of sandy outwash plains on the east side contributes to this distribution pattern as well but Jack Pine also grows quite often on expanses of virtually bare rock. The two kinds of sites, while seemingly quite different, do have at least two things in common—extremely low soil fertility and very poor ability to retain moisture.

Jack Pine is like the other pines with regard to its requirement for exposed mineral soil for the establishment of seedlings and the seedlings are even more demanding of direct sunlight for growth and survival. This species, like the others therefore, requires for its regeneration conditions that, in nature, are only created on any appreciable scale by forest fires. Jack Pine carries this dependence on fire on to an even more sophisticated level than the other two pines. With White Pine and Red Pine, some seed is produced almost every year and excellent crops are produced every three to seven years. The chances of a good seed crop, or any seed crop, coinciding with a forest fire, however, are very slight—which means that most seeds produced by these two species are wasted. The same is partly true with Jack Pine because some cones open and release seed whether or not conditions are appropriate. Many more cones, however, remain on the tree and stay tightly closed for as long as 25 years, waiting for the right moment. That, of course, is the arrival of a forest fire. Not only does the fire prepare a good seed bed and kill off the old trees, but also its heat causes the cones to open up and release the long imprisoned seed. Through this marvellous adaptation to fire, Jack Pine does not uselessly throw away its seeds but saves them until the time when they will really have a chance.

Red Pine
Pinus resinosa
Pin rouge

From a distance Red Pine may sometimes be confused with White Pine. With practice, however, you will come to appreciate that Red Pine foliage tends to be arranged in rather coarse, globular clusters whereas that of White Pine has a distinctly layered, much more "feathery" appearance. Of course, if you are close enough to see the platy pinkish bark (as opposed to the furrowed black bark of a mature White Pine) there won't be any doubt that the tree is a Red Pine. A final clincher is that Red Pine needles, although equally long as, or longer than, those of the other species, are borne in clusters of two—not five as in White Pine.

Red Pine is largely confined to sandy, well-drained soils and for this reason is very characteristic of the outwash plains on Algonquin's east side, but is rather scarce on the west side. Even in the west it is usually found in small pockets of outwash material (such as the campgrounds at Two Rivers, Mew Lake, and Pog Lake). Only very rarely does Red Pine grow on thin till over bedrock along south or west facing lake or bog edges where light levels are sufficiently high to maintain it.

It is almost a certainty that any stand of Red Pine that you see got its start from a forest fire. Seeds may germinate but do not grow under dense shrubs or on heavy sod or leaf litter. A forest fire reduces the surface litter, often exposing the mineral soil. In these conditions and with lots of light, Red Pine will germinate. With anything less than two thirds of natural sunlight, in fact, Red Pine seedlings start to suffer. Fairly obviously, it takes a forest fire to eliminate the brush, expose the mineral soil, and get rid of most overhead trees—to meet the requirements, in other words, for the establishment or regeneration of a stand of Red Pine.

Red Pine seeds showing tiny wings that aid in their (wind-assisted) dispersal

You may question just how reliable this dependence on forest fires could be but it must be kept in mind that, once established, Red Pine can live for a very long time indeed. The large Red Pine in the nature reserve zone on the east shore of Dickson Lake, for example, are now about 350 years old—perhaps the oldest known living things in the Park. Once a Red Pine has its place in the sun very little can harm it. The species is unusually resistant to insect and fungal attack and older trees may even survive forest fires that are not overly hot. Scars left by previous fires on the growth rings of old Red Pine, in fact, are very useful for determining just how frequently forest fires occurred here in Algonquin before modern man arrived on the scene. One study, carried out in the Greenleaf Lake area on the Park's east side, established that fires occurred in that area on the average once every 80 or 90 years. At that rate, quite obviously, Red Pine would never become extinct while waiting for the next forest fire necessary to launch the succeeding generation of seedlings.

Tamaracks grow in the parts of bogs closest to open water

The same Tamarack in summer...

... and fall

Before needle drop

Needles grow singly and in clusters

Old cones

Two male cones (lower side) and one female cone (above)

John Hickie

John Hickie

John Hickie

Algonquin Park Museum

Michael Runtz

Harry A. Thomson

8

Tamarack

Larix laricina

Mélèze laricin

The Tamarack, or larch, is famous as the only conifer native to eastern North America which turns colour (to gold) and sheds all its needles each fall. It is highly unconventional in many more ways than this, however.

For example, it grows in an amazingly wide range of soil types, ranging from the bogs most people associate it with, through gravel, to exposed bedrock. Its real requirement is good oxygenation for its roots, a condition which is obviously met on well-drained, upland soils but even in wet, lowland sites so long as the water is moving. This is one of the reasons why Tamarack grows well near the edges of boggy rivers but is replaced by Black Spruce farther back from the water.

Tamarack also requires full sunlight but rarely has this need fulfilled except in newly formed bogs. It is often the very first species to invade such areas but, even there, it is eventually relegated to fringe status. Not only does Tamarack require the moving water found only near the edge of a bog mat but also the seedlings simply cannot grow in the shade of their parents. The result is that the bulk of Tamarack stands in bogs are taken over by Black Spruce, a species which is more tolerant of shade and the stagnant, acid waters found in the main body of a bog.

The foliage of Tamaracks is a pleasing, light green colour and, on close examination, the needles will be seen to fall into two distinct patterns. On the very tips of the branches, the needles are borne singly along the twigs the way spruce needles are. Farther back, however, the needles appear in clusters somewhat in the manner of pine needles except that the clusters contain a much higher, and variable number (10 to 50) of needles and they sprout out of little woody knobs growing on the twig. In actual fact, the woody knobs are themselves twigs—dwarf twigs that grow so slowly that all the needles, which would otherwise be stretched out over the length of the twig, are jammed together, giving the appearance of a cluster. The dwarf twigs persist on the tree during the winter, as do the tiny cones, and this makes identification of Tamaracks simple even when the needles are absent.

The shedding of Tamarack needles is of more than passing interest. Foliage contains a high proportion of the nutrients essential for plant life and the advantage conifers normally have over deciduous trees is that by retaining their leaves they also retain the nutrients. This is particularly useful in nutrient-poor areas like bogs and indeed, even many of the broad-leaved shrubs in such areas are evergreen—as well as the needle-leaved conifers. The question, then, is how do Tamaracks do so well in bogs even when they "throw away" their nutrient-rich needles every year? We already know that Tamaracks growing at the edges of river bogs have their roots bathed in moving water which can supply the trees with nutrients unavailable farther back in the bog. There is an additional factor as well, however, and that is the close association formed between Tamarack roots and certain mushrooms. The roots of many trees but particularly conifers are typically surrounded and penetrated by the fine, threadlike tissues of soil fungi and it is believed that both trees and fungi benefit. The trees get nutrients from the fungi and the fungi get sugars from the tree. Normally, of course, we cannot see any of these goings-on but in the fall, when the fungi produce the visible, surface structures known as mushrooms, we sometimes get a few hints. The ground near Tamarack trees is an excellent place to look for fall mushrooms and, with some species, it is the only place to look. The Tamaracks and the mushrooms are partners in a very interesting success story.

White Spruce

Picea glauca

Épinette blanche Photos page 10

The White Spruce is a very widespread species, having the largest range of any tree found in Canada. It is just as much part of the scene in Newfoundland as it is in the Rocky Mountains or near the edge of the tundra in the Northwest Territories. In spite of this success, however, White Spruce seldom dominates the landscape in the sense of forming large, pure stands. Here in Algonquin, for example, it grows in a variety of moist, though well-drained, situations but almost always in association with other tree species. It is typically found with aspen and White Birch but it also mixes in with Balsam Fir, White Pine, and Red Pine and it may even grow in company with Yellow Birch in the moister, lower reaches of the Park's west side hardwood forests.

It is relatively tolerant of shade and can grow up under a canopy of aspen, for example, but it does especially well in sunny, open conditions. There, it may reach imposing heights of 20-25 metres and this, along with a pleasing, conical form, can make the White Spruce a particularly impressive tree.

Wherever it grows, however, and no matter how successful an individual White Spruce has been in its life, like all trees, it faces a major problem in trying to reproduce itself. The difficulty to put it in human terms, is that trees not only lack the ability to care for their offspring but also they are unable to see where good nearby growing sites might be, let along actually get their seeds to those sites. The less than ideal solution evolved by many trees is to produce thousands of very small seeds and depend on the chance that some of them will flutter down to a suitable location and eventually become mature trees.

The White Spruce follows this basic plan but the details and the complications encountered in making it work are well worth considering. In mid-May, high up on mature trees (and therefore in places hard for human observers to see), White Spruce produces two kinds of flowers called male and female conelets. The male flowers do not last long and disintegrate soon after discharging their pollen which is blown in the wind to female flowers on the same or different trees. These female flowers enlarge over the summer to become green cones (about 5 cm long in the case of White Spruce) and then ripen (turning brown in the process) in late August or early September. The seeds, hidden under the cone scales at two per scale or about 130 per cone, are only about 2 millimetres long (although they also have a thin wing attached to the seed to aid in dispersal from the parent tree). It takes about 530,000 White Spruce seeds to weigh a kilogram and even a big tree with over 10,000 cones would rarely produce even half that number of healthy, viable seeds. Notwithstanding their small size, however, the seeds are loaded with food reserves—they have to be if they are going to get new spruce trees started to life—and that is where the real troubles start.

Anything nutritious is a target for hungry mouths and, to have any chance of producing surviving seeds, White Spruce and the other conifers have evolved (partly successful) defences. One obvious defence is the cone scales which do succeed in keeping most birds at bay. They are not successful, however, in warding off Red Squirrels which clip off bushels of cones and then rip them apart without much trouble. Nor are they immune to attacks by the White-winged Crossbill, a colourful pink, black, and white finch whose specialized bill (quite literally crossed at the tip) is used to pry open the cone scales so that the seeds can then be plucked out with the tongue.

There is a defence against these creatures as well, however. In most years, White Spruce trees in a given area produce very few cones and seeds. The local squirrels eke out a living by eating probably every one that is produced and any crossbills around find the pickings so slim that they move on to other areas. This pattern results in very few or no new spruce seedlings but it also makes things very tough for the seed eaters and their numbers are kept very low. Then, about once in every 4 to 6 years, in response to poorly understood factors, all the White Spruce over a huge area will simultaneously produce tremendous cone crops. It is a paradise for the seed eaters but their numbers are so low (because of the previous poor crops) that they don't even come close to eating all the seeds. The White-winged Crossbills make the best try at it and, when the Park has a good White Spruce seed year, the numbers of these nomadic birds quickly build up into the tens, if not hundreds, of thousands. The air is filled with

Michael Runtz

John Hickie

A typical White Spruce

The pale, fine-scaled bark of a mature tree

Alan G. Gordon

Alan G. Gordon

Alan G. Gordon

Male flower

Female flowers and season's new shoots

Old cones

Alan G. Gordon

John Hickie

Michael Runtz

Red Spruce with "pagoda-like" upswept branches

Red Spruce bark

Twigs of Red Spruce (top), Black Spruce (middle), and White Spruce (bottom)

John Hickie

John Hickie

Black Spruce at edge of bog

Typical stand of Black Spruce

John Hickie

Michael Runtz

Inside a Black Spruce forest

Old cones of Black Spruce

Michael Runtz

Alan G. Gordon

Seeds in sectioned cone

Alan G. Gordon

Alan G. Gordon

Female flowers (cones) of Red Spruce

Old cones

Red Spruce laden with cones

John Hickie

Balsam Fir against fall foliage

Spire-shaped crowns of Balsam

John Hickie

John Hickie

Resin blisters in Balsam bark

Balsam needles are flat

Michael Runtz

Michael Runtz

Fertilized female flowers maturing into cones

Michael Runtz

Maturing cones

Mary I. Moore

Young male cones of Balsam

MNR (CSB)

12 Balsam-eating budworm is a major agent of change in the forest

Mary I. Moore

Seeds exposed in disintegrating cone

Central shafts of spent cones

Mary I. Moore

their calls and songs as they swirl from one heavily laden spruce top to the next and reap the bountiful harvest. They even go so far as to nest and raise young in the middle of winter if the crop is rich enough, and still they fail to get all the seeds. The squirrels and the birds have prospered but the spruce trees, although they haven't exactly defeated their enemies, have at least overwhelmed them and produced seeds that will make it through the gauntlet of seed eaters.

Spruce Identification Aids

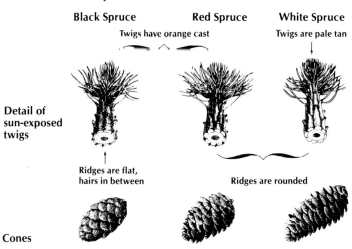

Black Spruce
Twigs have orange cast

Red Spruce

White Spruce
Twigs are pale tan

Detail of sun-exposed twigs

Ridges are flat, hairs in between

Ridges are rounded

Cones

Black Spruce
Picea mariana
Épinette noire   **Photos page 11**

It must be admitted that most people find the Black Spruce to be a distinctly uninspiring tree. Especially compared to White Spruce, this species seems to come second in just about every department. In form, the Black Spruce is usually best described as scraggly; it rarely grows more than 15 metres tall in Algonquin, with 10 metres being far more typical; its branches are small, short, and drooping; its needles are often only a centimetre long; the cones are puny; and even the seeds are tiny by comparison with White Spruce.

Nevertheless, Black Spruce is by no means an insignificant tree. Farther north, it covers vast areas and is the foundation of Canada's pulp and paper industry—Canada's biggest, and by far its most important earner of foreign exchange. Here in Algonquin, Black Spruce is not economically important and it is largely confined to bogs and outwash deposits—but this only points out another way in which this tree is truly remarkable.

The soil in bogs is based not on glacial till or sand, but on peat, the partly decayed remains of sedges and mosses. The point is that all plants—and animals, too, for that matter—need certain chemicals, commonly called nutrients, for proper growth. Although some nutrients are transported to plants through the atmosphere, the more important source is the mineral soil in which most plants grow. By comparison, plants growing on peat find themselves in a sodden, non-mineral, nutrient-starved medium and they must depend on a diffuse circulation system that only very slowly brings in dissolved nutrients from surrounding areas. In addition, peaty soils are very acidic and distinctly cool and all these factors put severe limits on the kinds of plants that can exist in bogs and on how well they grow.

Given these realities, we should not look down on the Black Spruce but should marvel at its success instead. As a matter of fact, some of the supposedly modest features of the Black Spruce can be seen, on close examination, to be definite assets. Scraggly, drooping branches, for example, may not be beautiful to our eyes but their growth doesn't require a large investment from the nutritionally hard-pressed Black Spruce and they are well adapted to receiving heavy snow loads without breaking.

In its reproduction as well Black Spruce shows some fine tuning to existence in bogs. The fate of most seeds and seedlings in such areas is to get lost or smothered in the thick ground layers of sphagnum moss but Black Spruce has evolved another way. When the drooping lower branches touch and are enveloped in the moss layer they develop roots and eventually become new, neighbouring trees. In many bog situations this "layering" procedure apparently accounts for most Black Spruce reproduction.

The boggy islands and ribbons of Black Spruce lying in the lowlands of Algonquin add a strong northern flavour to the Park. They bring us the lonely beauty captured in Tom Thomson's famous canvas, *Northern River*, and also many of the plants and animals associated with the great boreal forests of Black Spruce found farther north. Birds like the Boreal Chickadee, Gray Jay, and Spruce Grouse, for example, are all strongly associated with Algonquin's Black Spruce forests and wouldn't be here without them.

Red Spruce
Picea rubens
Épinette rouge   **Photos pages 10 & 11**

The Red Spruce might be called Algonquin Park's mystery tree. It is certainly present, in isolated pockets scattered here and there across the southwestern highlands of the Park and in neighbouring Haliburton County, but many people, who know all the other trees perfectly well, are unaware that the Red Spruce is in our midst. Until the 1950s, in fact, even professional foresters in Ontario for the most part were unable to recognize Red Spruce and sometimes disputed its presence.

With a record like that, it might seem rather hopeless for a beginner to identify a Red Spruce with any confidence but it certainly can be done. Mature trees are actually very distinctive in several ways. Their crowns are wide, coming rather abruptly to a blunt point and the branches are far enough apart that, from a distance, the tree almost looks more like a hemlock than a spruce. White Spruce, with its smoothly tapering crown and thick branches that hide the trunk presents a quite different aspect and the spindly Black Spruce with its extremely narrow crown, is nothing at all like a Red Spruce. Other features useful in the identification of mature Red Spruce are that the branches often have a "pagoda-like" upsweep at the ends and that the bark is thick, black, and furrowed—more similar to that of a mature White Pine than to the thin, scaly, gray bark of a White Spruce. For small trees, or as the final clincher in the identification of large ones, the most useful feature is the fine structure of the twigs older than one year (i.e., back at least one branching from the tip—see diagram this page and photo on page 10).

Red Spruce is much more tolerant of shade than our other two spruces and it tends to be associated with Hemlock or Yellow Birch, sometimes near lakeshores but often in moist pockets surrounded by hardwood hills.

There is a feeling of damp lushness in a Red Spruce forest and this is a suggestive clue as to why Red Spruce is present in the Algonquin highlands, so far west, and cut off, from the species' main range in New England and the Maritimes. As discussed earlier, the greater elevations of Algonquin's west side result in a climate measurably cooler than that found in surrounding areas. The extra height makes for a wetter regime as well because it forces eastward moving air masses to lose rain or snow as they rise up over the highlands. The wetter and colder climate of Algonquin's west side is, in fact, remarkably similar to that encountered in many of the Appalachian strongholds of Red Spruce, which no doubt goes a long way towards explaining why it is here.

The structural differences between White Spruce (left) and Red Spruce (right) can be striking.

Flat needles and old cones

Seedling in shade of parent

Hemlocks have strong branches

Little grows in the shade of a Hemlock grove

John Hickie

John Hickie

John Hickie

Male cones at leaf tips

Developing cones

Stringy bark is characteristic

Shoreline Cedar showing distinct deer browse line

Mary I. Moore

Michael Runtz

Michael Runtz

Algonquin Park Museum

Balsam Fir

Abies balsamea

Sapin baumier   Photos page 12

Balsam Fir is a medium sized tree of low lying, moderately moist sites, seldom growing taller than the 12 to 18 metre range. From a distance it can be mistaken for White Spruce although it usually has a narrower, more conical shape. Seen closer up, the lower, shaded branches of Balsam Fir have needles that twist around from their radial attachment sites to end up lying in flat planes perpendicular to the light above. (Higher up in the trees, where the foliage is exposed to direct sunlight the needles project out from the twigs in all directions just the way they always do in the spruces.) The needles are flat and, unlike the four-sided needles of spruce, resist being rolled between two fingers. If present on the tree, cones are another real identification giveaway because in fir trees they point upwards from the branches rather than hanging down as in other conifers.

Balsam needles are the source of the beautiful fragrance so closely associated in the minds of many people with "the north woods", but the rest of the tree is notable for producing aromatic resinous chemicals as well. The otherwise smooth gray bark of young trees is dimpled with resin blisters and even the cones have their share of sticky, messy pitch. The purpose of the resins is not entirely understood although they do flow more copiously when a tree is being attacked by fungi and there is some evidence that cone resins help deter Red Squirrels and crossbills from extracting and eating the relatively large seeds.

Basically, though, if Balsam Fir's array of chemicals serves for defence, success has been rather poor. Some trees start to rot when they are only 40 years old and often half the trees are affected by the time they are 70. Moose have a taste for Balsam twigs and foliage, and in some parts of Algonquin, many Balsam trees have had their branches, up to Moose head height, pruned right back to the trunk.

Of all the eaters of Balsam Fir, however, the most important by far is the Spruce Budworm. Notwithstanding the name, Balsam is the preferred host of this insect, a small and drab grayish moth as an adult and a needle-eating caterpillar as a larva. The caterpillars attack the new growth of foliage as soon as it flushes out in late May or June and, when their numbers build up to high levels as they occasionally do, the effects can be quite striking. There are so many Budworm caterpillars available, for example, that insect-eating birds have unparalleled success. Many nest two or three times in a summer and some birds like the Cape May Warbler, rare in non-budworm years, build up to very high population levels.

Late spring frosts may arrest a budworm outbreak by killing larvae but otherwise it will last several year. Balsam needles normally stay on the tree for about four years so if budworms eat all the new growth for that many years in a row the trees will end up completely defoliated and die. This happened in many areas of Algonquin Park in the early 1970s. It should be seen as a normal occurrence in Balsam Fir stands—and indeed a central part of Balsam ecology. Apart from the temporary bonanza to birds during the outbreaks the ensuing death of the stand leads to increased light on the forest floor, more growth of shrubs, increased numbers of small rodents (and therefore their predators) and good feeding for deer and Moose. The Budworm, therefore, is an important link between the Balsam Fir and wildlife prosperity.

Eastern White Cedar

Thuja occidentalis

Thuya de l'Est

The Cedar is one Algonquin conifer that needs little introduction. The flattened, spreading foliage makes recognition very simple and most visitors are already familiar with the tree from back home.

As a matter of fact, Cedar is more suited to areas underlain by limestone rocks (as in southern agricultural Ontario, for example) than it is to the nutrient-poor, acidic soils of the Precambrian Shield. For this reason Cedar rarely dominates swamplands in Algonquin the way it does elsewhere. Instead it tends to grow around the edges of bogs and along lakeshores where the soil is moist but where there is also some lateral movement of groundwater to bring in new nutrients.

Cedar is well known as a highly palatable and nutritious deer food. Back in the days when Algonquin Park had a very high deer population it used to be a difficult, usually impossible, challenge to find a Cedar seedling, and along the lakeshores every Cedar's foliage was all browsed away below the height of a deer's head. This left a sharp, conspicuous division known as a "browse line" between the browsed lower branches and the untouched foliage above. With the decline of deer in the 1970s and their replacement by Moose (which browse Cedar much less) the pressure on Cedar has lessened and in many places browse lines have now become blurred or disappeared.

Eastern Hemlock

Tsuga canadensis

Pruche de l'est

Hemlock stands out from Algonquin's other conifers in a number of ways. The stout branches and wide crowns of mature trees are very different from those of spruce, Fir, and Tamarack. There is no possibility of confusion with our pines either because the flat needles of Hemlock are borne singly (on stalks) and are very short (only about one cm long) giving the foliage no resemblance at all to that of pines. Hemlock stands out also by growing in two distinct situations. It is a characteristic tree of lakeshore forests on the Park's west side, mixed in with other conifers such as Balsam, White Spruce, Cedar, and White Pine and also with Yellow Birch. In addition, however, it commonly grows in pure stands or groves well up on hillsides (often north-facing) and completely surrounded by deciduous forests of Sugar Maple.

It is known that Hemlock seedlings require cool, moist soil conditions for survival and this apparently explains local patterns of Hemlock growth. Lakeshores are obviously cool and moist and on hillsides the configuration of underlying bedrock occasionally brings water close enough to the surface to make conditions suitable for Hemlock seedlings.

Once a Hemlock seedling does get established and past its first year of life (when it is so small it can be dried out by direct sunlight or smothered by falling maple leaves) it is capable of extraordinary tenacity and resiliency. It can live on in almost complete shade and, although it may have negligible growth under such conditions, it is capable of responding quickly to changes which admit light through the overhead canopy. In the unlikely circumstance of full, direct light, Hemlock saplings have been known to grow as much as 45 cm in height in a single growing season and 10 cm in trunk diameter in a decade. Shaded saplings 200 years old and only a few cm in diameter after all that time are still capable of rapidly growing up and filling a hole left in the canopy by the death of an even older tree should they get the chance.

Stands of old-growth Hemlocks are aesthetically very pleasing with their rich brown, massive trunks rising up into dark green lacy foliage. Even on a hot summer day the air is cool and moist and, because of the deep shade down on the spongy forest floor, there is very little shrubbery to obstruct our view through the old trees.

These characteristics of Hemlock groves do more than merely please the human eye, however. The same spreading branches and thick foliage that cast such dense shade in summer also intercept much of the snow that falls in winter. The result is significantly lower snow depths in Hemlock stands. In bad winters this can be of crucial importance to White-tailed Deer, southern animals that bog down in snow deeper than 50 cm deep. Algonquin's Hemlock stands were probably a key factor in permitting deer to occupy Algonquin Park when logging and fires created large areas of good deer food in the latter part of the 1800s. When Hemlock itself is cut, however, it is rarely succeeded by other Hemlocks and many large areas in northern Haliburton and adjoining southwestern Algonquin lost all their Hemlocks around the turn of the century when the bark of these trees (in particular its tannin content) was in heavy demand for tanning leather. A further blow to deer came with extensive logging in the Park for Hemlock in the 1950s and 60s (the Toronto subway was built with Algonquin Hemlock shoring timbers, for example) and many authorities believe this was a major contributor to the demise of deer in the Park. Today, under the Algonquin Park Master Plan, the cutting of Hemlocks and other conifers is carefully controlled in the Park's remaining deer yards.

John Hickie

Silvery Largetooth Aspen in late spring

John Hickie

In silvery phase

Michael Runtz

In summer

John Hickie

Largetooth Aspens turn bright yellow in fall

Mary I. Moore

Two Trembling Aspen leaves; one of Largetooth

Algonquin Park Museum

Trembling Aspens

Dan Strickland

Trembling Aspens turn dull yellow in fall

John Hickie

Male flowers

Harry A. Thomson

Maturing female flowers

Mary I. Moore

Seeds about to depart

16

The Deciduous Trees

Largetooth Aspen
Populus grandidentata
Peuplier à grandes dents

Largetooth Aspen is very similar in aspect to Trembling Aspen although its bark often has a distinctly yellowish cast and a close look at the leaves will show unmistakable, large, scalloped serrations along the edges—making identification easy. On average it prefers drier, better drained sites than Trembling Aspen but, in practice, both species are often found together. This, plus the fact that they look so much alike, leads most people to lump them together as aspens or "poplars" and leave it at that. There are two times of the year, however, when the aspens appear very different. In the spring, Trembling Aspen flowers and leafs out a full two weeks earlier than Largetooth Aspen. Moreover, the leaves of the latter species, when unfolding, have a downy underside that is exposed to view, giving the whole tree a silvery or snowy appearance. This contrasts strikingly with the pastel greens of nearby Trembling Aspens that have already leafed out and makes the separation of the two species a simple and eye-pleasing exercise, even from miles away. Soon afterwards the two trees melt into the same summer greenery but in early October they again pop out of the landscape in very different ways. The leaves of Largetooth Aspen turn colour first, becoming a brilliant golden orange and about a week later Trembling Aspen follows suit—but with distinctly more sombre, flat yellows.

Of the 34 tree species listed in this book all but seven follow the same pattern in having individual trees that are both male and female at the same time. There may well be—in fact usually are—quite separate male, pollen-producing flowers and female, seed-producing flowers, but both kinds of flowers are found on the same tree. With this arrangement, a tree's female flowers can be fertilized by pollen produced by another tree nearby or by pollen that comes from the same tree's own male flowers. The advantage, of course, for such "bisexual" trees is that even an isolated individual can get by without a partner and still produce seeds. The disadvantage is that the individuals growing from such seeds will be near duplicates of the parent tree and have a poorer chance of coming up with a new genetic combination that might be able to compete just a little bit more effectively.

Red Maple and the three species of ash in Algonquin Park are usually different from this normal pattern of sex in trees and the three species of poplar always are. That is, there is no such thing as a bisexual poplar. There are poplars with male flowers only and there are poplars that are pure female—but nothing in between. With many tree species the reasons for such departures from tree orthodoxy are not understood but in the poplars there is at least a plausible explanation.

In the Largetooth Aspen, for example, the system of separate sexes necessarily means that fertilization of female flowers is by pollen from a different tree and this means that the seeds will always be genetically variable—with no chance at all of being just identical copies of the parents. Normally the risk of such a system would be that the female flowers might not be pollinated at all—for lack of a sufficiently close male tree. However, the Largetooth Aspen and other poplars have a highly efficient system for producing exact copies of themselves without resorting to sex at all. They do it by sending up suckers from their root systems. Each sucker is nourished by the parent tree's root stem and is capable of becoming a new tree in its own right (albeit as an exact genetic copy of its male, or female, parent). Aspens are capable, in other words, of "cloning" themselves and often all the aspen trees covering an area of an acre or even more are copies of the same original individual. So efficient is this means of reproduction that many aspen trees are believed to originate as root suckers and relatively few start out from seeds. It is still worthwhile producing seeds, however, not only because they are new genetic combinations, but also because they are transported by wind to remote areas, far beyond the reach of existing aspen root systems, and which are occasionally suitable for new aspen colonies.

Thus the separate-sex aspens have the best of all worlds. They can always reproduce themselves—and with dramatic efficiency at that—through their root suckering system. And, if there are trees of the opposite sex nearby, seeds can be produced with the maximum potential for genetic variability and no chance that the seeds will merely repeat the exact genetic duplication already accomplished through suckering.

Trembling Aspen
Populus tremuloides
Peuplier faux-tremble (Tremble)

The Trembling Aspen is a common and important tree in Algonquin and yet many Park visitors mistake it for White Birch. The confusion arises from the white bark of the aspen although, in fact, it is rarely so bright a white as birch bark and it has none of the birch's papery quality.

Fortunately for people just learning their trees, it is often possible to make direct comparisons because the two species have similar requirements and often grow in the same places. Both trees are "pioneer" species which must have full sunlight to survive. Like the White Birch, therefore, the aspen can only be expected to grow in areas where the former tree cover has been removed by some major disturbance such as fire or violent windstorm. Even then, the aspen will only grow in that location for one generation (failing yet another forest-destroying event) because its own shade will make life impossible for any small aspen trees on the forest floor below. As with White Birch, the fact that the aspen is a common tree in spite of its absolute dependence on repeated major disturbances, underscores just how common those disturbances must be in the natural forest.

When its extreme, though simple, requirements are met, the Trembling Aspen does very well. It grows with astonishing rapidity and may well pass 15 metres in height by the time it is 30 years old and 25 metres when it is 70. By then its intense life (for a tree) is more than half over—although this should not be taken to mean that the aspen is therefore a minor, or passing element in the forest scene.

Perhaps in part because it always grows in conditions of direct sunlight, the Trembling Aspen is extremely nutritious and probably no other tree surpasses it in importance to wildlife. The buds are an important winter food for Ruffed Grouse; the twigs of young trees are avidly eaten by deer and Moose; and the bark is consumed by mice, Snowshoe Hares, Porcupines, and Beavers (for whom it is the most preferred tree species). One study showed that just one acre of aspen could support a colony of five Beavers for up to three years. The leaves, too, are very important and it surprises most people that by far the most important food for Black Bears in May and June is the tasty new foliage of aspens. The bears go right up into the tree tops to get it.

Not surprisingly, insects also find the Trembling Aspen to be good eating and over 300 kinds are known to feed on it. One species, the Forest Tent Caterpillar, periodically builds up to epidemic proportions and defoliates aspens over large areas but it is actually rather remarkable that such events do not occur more frequently. After all, insects have tremendous reproductive rates and the leaves can't exactly get away, so why do so few aspen leaves normally fall prey to those 300 different insect enemies? The answer is that the leaves of aspen (and other trees) defend themselves with chemicals. The year's first flush of leaves usually do not have many of these natural insecticides (the odd cold night often will kill off any attackers "for free" at that time of year) but, later on, the leaves start to produce a succession of different chemicals that usually keep the various would-be leaf-eaters at bay. And, when the numbers of attackers do start to build up, aspens have the ability to increase their defences. The concentration of poisonous compounds called phenols in still undamaged leaves can double in just three days when nearby leaves are subjected to a major attack. This occurs whether the attacked leaves are on the same or separate, nearby trees. Apparently damaged leaves release volatile chemicals that float through the air and trigger the build up of defensive insecticides in any nearby aspen leaves whether or not they are on the same tree.

John Hickie

John Hickie

John Hickie

John Hickie

Bronzy leaves

Balsam Poplar

Male flowers

Female flowers

Dan Strickland

John Hickie

John Hickie

John Hickie

White Birches, Costello Lake

Purple "halos" surround leafless White Birches

Leaves of White Birch

Peter Smith

Papery bark of White Birch

18

Upright female flowers (left) and hanging male flowers (right)

Balsam Poplar
Populus balsamifera
Peuplier baumier

Balsam Poplar is found right across Canada including the far north and on into Alaska. In Algonquin it is rather uncommon, being found here and there as individual trees or small groves, more commonly on the east side and often in gravelly, alluvial soils near rivers.

It has a long straight trunk with a narrow crown of widely spaced ascending branches. The bark is smooth and greenish in young trees but later turns dark gray and develops rough, vertical ridges giving an appearance quite unlike the Park's other two native poplar species, the Trembling and Largetooth Aspens.

Balsam Poplar is noteworthy for its sticky, resinous twigs and for the spectacular production of seeds by the female trees in late June. Poplar seeds are extremely tiny and, unique among Park trees, carry long white hairs that serve to buoy them up and permit the breezes to carry them far away from their points of origin. In the Balsam Poplar so many seeds are produced that, for a time, the trees, and everything nearby, seem to be covered by a summer "snowstorm". It is no accident that the poplars have evolved such light, airborne seeds. These trees are so intolerant of shade that the seeds must land in new treeless areas where there is full sunlight if they are to have any possibility of success. Such areas are few and far between and evolution has therefore favoured a seed dispersal system that maximized the chances of finding them.

White Birch
Betula papyrifera
Bouleau blanc

White Birch is a tree that is immediately familiar to everyone. The distinctly papery, and often brilliant white, bark makes the tree a real standout. Then too, it is famous as the source of material for the birch bark canoes used by the Algonquin Indians.

White Birch also has some interesting lessons to teach us about the true nature of forests in this and many other parts of the world. Very often it is assumed that before modern man began to "interfere", forests lived on through the centuries, virtually unchanged. Only once in a long while did an ancient forest giant come crashing to the ground, to be quickly replaced by another similar tree. And, down on the forest floor, the abundant wildlife lived as it always had among the cathedral-like pillars of tree trunks rising hundreds of feet into the air. Indeed, Alexander Kirkwood, a Scottish expatriate who helped establish Algonquin Park back in 1893, wrote, while referring to the Park forests: "The noble pines and stately oaks bespeak the growth of centuries. The rooks caw from their hereditary nests in the tree tops and the wind sounds solemnly in their branches."

Even today, such statements would be entirely in keeping with the way many people believe a natural forest operates. But quite apart from the fact that Algonquin Park has never had any rooks or anything resembling a "stately" oak, Mr. Kirkwood's statement missed the mark in at least one, very important way. Even before the white man arrived on the scene, the "primeval" forests of North America were in a state of flux and the White Birch is an excellent illustration of this fact.

Here is a rapidly growing tree that rarely lives to be 150 years old and absolutely must have full sunlight. The White Birch, in other words, did not—and indeed, could not—grow in the towering primeval forests romanticized by Kirkwood and many others. It was always present as a "fringe" species around lakeshores where enough light was admitted from the "water" side, but the only places where it did really well were sunny, open areas whose previous tree cover had been removed. Before modern man arrived on the scene the only agents capable of doing this were fires (usually started by lightning) or (more rarely) violent windstorms. The interesting—and instructive—point is that White Birch was and is an extremely common tree in the huge area stretching from Newfoundland to Alaska. It therefore follows that forest fires (or violent winds) must have been routinely destroying forests all over this area or otherwise White Birch simply would not have been here. It is also hard to imagine why White Birch and several other species (the aspens and Jack Pine, for example) would have become adapted to the conditions created by these destructive agents unless these destructive agents were a reasonably common and normal part of the "primeval" scene.

This is all the more apparent when you realize that, in many cases, the White Birch trees that colonized a burned-over area, for example, could only live there for one generation. They would then be succeeded by other species such as White Spruce or Balsam Fir. This is because White Birch seedlings are so intolerant of shade that they cannot grow beneath their own parents.

If White Birch has such a temporary and precarious hold on the land and is yet such a common tree, we have to revise our thoughts about how permanent the forest primeval really was.

Yellow Birch
Betula alleghaniensis
Bouleau jaune (Merisier)   Photos page 20

The Yellow Birch is a common tree in Algonquin's west side hardwood forests but it often goes unrecognized by Park visitors. The bark of young trees looks more or less the way you would expect—thin and papery with an unmistakably yellowish hue— but older trees are entirely different. Here the trunks are covered with thick, gray or black, irregular plates and only by looking up into the smaller branches of the crown can you see remnants of the juvenile yellowish papery bark.

Once you know what to look for, however, you will start to realize how impressive these trees can be. The largest Yellow Birch in Ontario, for example, is located near Harry Lake in the southern part of the Park. It measures 31 metres tall and 114 cm in diameter.

It would be wrong to assume, however, that large size, old age (up to 300 years), and reasonable abundance necessarily mean that the Yellow Birch has found a sure-fire formula for success. In fact, it would be more accurate to say that just about every Yellow Birch tree you see is something of a fluke. Yellow Birch produces millions of very tiny seeds that are released during the winter and dispersed over large areas by being blown across the snow crust. This would be all very well except for one thing. Sugar Maple lives in virtually the same soil and moisture conditions that are most suitable for Yellow Birch and the flattened layer of Sugar Maple leaves on the forest floor is an almost impenetrable barrier for tiny young Yellow Birch seedlings. The vast majority of Yellow Birch seedlings perish when they fail to get their roots down to the mineral soil below. Even when they do succeed, they are often smothered by the following year's Sugar Maple leaf fall.

About the only places a Yellow Birch seed has any chance of success are moist, lower slopes or seepage areas where Sugar Maple doesn't do so well or on the tops of rotting logs or stumps—where breezes will clear off those lethal dead maple leaves. In the hardwood forests of Algonquin Park a high percentage of Yellow Birch trees get their start on such fortuitous seedbeds of rotting wood. Even though the original support entirely disappears afterwards the "perched birch" is left standing on the stilt-like support roots that once grew down the sides of the stump or log. In other cases, present day Yellow Birch trees may owe their origin to autumn leaf fires that eliminated the local maple seedling competition, burned off the layer of dead maple leaves, and exposed the soil long enough for delicate Yellow Birch seedlings to get established.

Even then, survival would not be assured unless there was greater than normal amounts of sunlight coming through the overhead canopy (otherwise the seedlings would be outcompeted by young Sugar Maples). The seedlings would also have to escape being eaten by deer which find the wintergreen flavour of Yellow Birch very much to their liking. In the heyday of Algonquin's White-tailed Deer herd, from the late 1800s to the early 1960s, it is believed that Yellow Birch regeneration in the Park was virtually non-existent. Now that deer have become scarce in the Park once again, Yellow Birch seedlings have at least a slight chance to get permanently established. It is interesting to note in this regard that the presence in Algonquin of large Yellow Birch 150-250 years old almost certainly means that deer were rare or absent back when those trees were getting started.

Michael Runtz

Dan Strickland

A Yellow Birch in summer

The same tree changing colour in fall

John Hickie

John Hickie

Alan G. Gordon

Life began on a stump

Young bark

Bark of an old tree

Mary I. Moore

John Hickie

Michael Runtz

Male (left) and female flowers

Two tiny seedlings

Yellow Birch leaves

Patches of rusty foliage in late fall betray the presence of Red Oak on south facing hillsides

John Hickie

Red Oak in summer

John Hickie

Before leaf-out

John Hickie

Red Oak leaves have sharp points

John Hickie

Leaves and flowers appear together

Tiny, one year old acorn and current male flowers

John Hickie

Acorns take two summers to develop

John Hickie

21

Red Oak
Quercus rubra
Chêne rouge

Bur Oak
Quercus macrocarpa
Chêne à gros fruits

Speckled Alder
Alnus rugosa
Aune commun

North America's many species of oak trees are normally associated with warmer and drier climates than that found in Algonquin. Even the Red Oak, which, for an oak, is a "hardy northerner", has the same basic preferences. Even though Red Oak is a common, even dominant, tree only 15-25 km southwest of the Park (as in the Dwight and Dorset areas) and also on Algonquin's warmer and drier east side, things are very different in the Park's western uplands. The greater altitude makes conditions sufficiently colder and wetter that Red Oak almost entirely drops out of the picture. Only occasional, small pockets of oak grow in the Highway 60 area of the Park, for example, and then usually only on rocky, southwest-facing, ridge tops that have warmer than normal microclimates because they receive the direct rays of the afternoon sun. Clearly, the Red Oak is a basically southern tree that is reaching the limits of its tolerance here in Algonquin and is greatly affected even by the apparently subtle climatic differences existing between the two main regions within our Park boundaries.

Most visitors are unaware of Red Oak and its pattern of distribution in Algonquin because the trees are mostly high up on hilltops where people don't often go and, from a distance, green summer oaks don't stand out from other tree species. In the fall, however, it is an easy matter to detect the presence of oaks. Maples and other hardwoods lose their leaves in early October and then the more persistent, reddish brown fall foliage of the oaks makes them easily visible, even to far-off hikers and canoeists, for the rest of the month.

The fact that Red Oak is so much more prevalent on Algonquin's east side may be hard to detect at most times of the year but it is of great significance. The acorns produced by Red Oak are among the most nutritious and abundant fall foods available to wildlife. Deer feed heavily on ripe acorns that have fallen to the forest floor and bears don't even wait for that. They go right up into the trees instead, and there they often do severe damage when they break off branches to bring acorns within reach. Tangled messes of broken branches (so-called "bear's nests") are left afterwards, just as often happens in Beech trees. Many authorities believe that Red Oak acorns are critically important for bears as they fatten up for hibernation and it may be more than just a coincidence that bears seem to be more common on Algonquin's east side—where oak stands are common—than they are on the west side.

Algonquin has a second, but very rare species of oak known only from the Barron Canyon on the east side of Algonquin and from the Squirrel Rapids area farther downstream on the Barron River. This is the Bur Oak, a species with smoothly lobed leaves. Its rarity here can be explained by its strong preference for clay-based soils which are almost totally lacking in the Park.

Red Oak photos preceding page, Bur Oak opposite.

Speckled Alder is the small, deciduous tree that grows in great profusion in creek bottoms, around lakes, beaver ponds, bogs or in almost any other place with moist soil. It is very much a part of Algonquin although some might dispute its inclusion in a book on our trees. It seldom reaches eight metres in height and the small sprawling trunks are, at most, 15 cm in diameter. Among its few striking features are the globular female flowers which, over summer, mature into hard, woody structures strongly resembling the cones of evergreen trees and serving the same purpose—the protection of developing seeds (technically called nutlets) held between the cone scales. The cones persist on the tree several years after the seeds have been released and this makes identification very easy. They are the only broad-leaved trees in Algonquin with cones.

The male flowers are in catkins which, on warm sunny days in April, swell dramatically into yellow, russet, and purple garlands festooning the alder swamps and releasing golden puffs of pollen when jostled by the breeze or passing animals. It is one of the first and most subtly beautiful signs of spring in Algonquin.

A greater importance of the Speckled Alder, however, lies with tiny swellings on its rootlets. These house bacteria which have the ability to take nitrogen out of the air and incorporate it into chemical compounds that can be used by plants. Every living thing (us included) needs nitrogen to make the proteins which, among other things, serve as the chemical machinery (enzymes) which facilitates all life processes. Animals get their supply by eating other animals or from plants. Most plants, in turn, get their nitrogen, not from the obvious source which is the nitrogen gas making up 80% of our atmosphere, but from rather scarce chemical compounds in the soil. Sometimes the soil is so poor in these nitrogen-containing compounds that the growth of plants is severely limited. That is why a plant (like the Speckled Alder) has a tremendous competitive advantage over other plants if it can enter into a partnership with bacteria having the ability to tap into the abundant nitrogen contained in air. This explains the notoriously rapid growth of alders, even in sandy sterile soils, but there are far-reaching beneficial consequences for other plants and animals as well.

For example, alder leaves are four times richer in nitrogen than the leaves of other plants. When they fall into our creeks and rivers each autumn, as billions upon billions of them do, those drab, seemingly inconsequential alder leaves bring a vitally important contribution of nitrogen that will make itself felt throughout the entire aquatic food chain. Insect larvae graze upon the nutritious leaves and they in turn support larger, predatory insects and minnows which form the food base of Algonquin's prized Brook Trout.

The same sort of thing holds true when alder leaves—or the dead trees themselves—fall on land. They fertilize the soil and make subsequent plant and animal growth far more luxurious than it would otherwise be.

This is basically why the Speckled Alder is so tremendously important in the ecology of Algonquin Park, but there are other impacts as well. If you come to the Park in October when Beavers are completing their winter food piles, you will see that the majority are comprised mostly or even entirely of Speckled Alder. Alder is not the preferred winter food of Beavers but, being so abundant and fast-growing, it is by far the most important here in Algonquin and without a doubt responsible for the Beaver's local prosperity.

Another impact stems from the fact that alders cover big tracts of land and constitute a definite habitat. As with maple forests, spruce bogs, and other Park habitats, alder swamps have their own complement of smaller plants, insects, and animals that never or seldom live anywhere else. There is, for example, the Alder Flycatcher that lives exclusively in alder creek bottoms and the gorgeous Golden-winged Warbler, although rare here in the Park, very often has the same preference.

The Speckled Alder may not be our idea of a beautiful tree but it should be everyone's idea of an important one.

A second species of alder, the Green Alder (*Alnus crispa*) is found on lakeshores on the east side of Algonquin.

Dan Strickland

Bur Oak tree

Mary I. Moore

Acorns have burs and leaves have rounded lobes

John Hickie

Typical stand of Speckled Alder in a creek bottom

John Hickie

Leaves and speckled bark

Dan Strickland

Flowers before leaf-out in spring

Michael Runtz

Alder "cone"

John Hickie

Female (upper left) and male flowers

Michael Runtz

Alder root nodules

23

American Beech

Fagus grandifolia

Hêtre à grandes feuilles

The Beech is a common tree in Algonquin's west side hardwood forests and one that is easily recognized by most people. The beautiful, smooth, pale gray bark immediately sets it apart from other trees and, especially in very large individuals, the old sculpted limbs impart a sense of gnarled timelessness that is very appealing.

Beech trees can live three or four times as long as a human being and some even last for over 400 years. Nevertheless, the long lives of big Beech trees can be misleading. To begin with, every big Beech tree is a "one in a million" survivor from a vast number of potential trees that started out in life at the same time. For each seed that lands in a good site, many more have the misfortune of germinating in places that are too wet, or too dry, or too shady, or too sunny—or have something else that isn't right for young Beech seedlings. The great majority of Beech seeds, in fact, barely get started before they come to grief. The situation is slightly better with suckers, erect shoots growing up around an established tree from its shallow root system. Because they are still connected to, and nourished by, the parent tree, the suckers can often withstand more severe conditions than true seedlings and sometimes they form dense thickets of potential new trees.

No matter how a Beech tree gets established, its future is far from guaranteed. Its chief problem will be the shade of the forest canopy above and, even if it can live for a long time in deep shade, it won't grow and has no chance of long term success unless one of the big trees shading it falls down and lets in the sun. Even then, there won't be room for all the contenders and competition among all the available young Beech trees will be severe. Worse, Beech trees are not alone in the race to fill the vacant hole in the canopy. A young Sugar Maple may well be the eventual winner.

Assuming a Beech tree does make it up into the canopy, however, it still isn't home-free. The thin skin of Beech trees is highly susceptible to injury and spores of wood-rotting fungi may enter through the smallest wound and sap the vigour of the struggling tree. There is even a parasitic flower called Beechdrops whose roots attach themselves to the roots of Beech trees and siphon off the trees' energy. (These strange little plants—which have no need for chlorophyll the way normal plants do—appear above ground and briefly flower in late August. They stand about a foot high and are yellowish brown in colour.)

If all this wasn't enough, there is one more obstacle to Beech tree prosperity. When Beeches are between 40 to 60 years old they start to produce, at irregular intervals of a few years, large crops of beechnuts, called "mast" or "beechmast". Beechnuts are big, edible, and nutritious and, in fact, the scientific name of our Beech tree, *Fagus grandifolia*, comes from a Greek word, *phago*, meaning "to eat". To the tree, the advantage of a big seed is that the resulting seedling will be big and vigorous and have a good chance of getting its root down through the thick layer of dead leaves on the forest floor. (This is a much bigger problem than you might think and some other trees, like Yellow Birch for example, whose seeds are very tiny, only become established when the seeds happen to fall on exposed mineral soil or perhaps a moss mat on a rotting log or stump.)

There is, however, a very heavy price that Beech trees must pay for producing big, nutritious seeds. Good food attracts hungry mouths and big crops of ripening beechnuts are highly popular with Black Bears. The bears do not wait for the nuts to fall, however; they go right up the trees after them (often leaving characteristic claw scars on the trunks). The loss of beechnuts would be bad enough but the bears, being so heavy, cannot directly reach the beechnuts out at the ends of the branches so, instead, they install themselves in some convenient crotch in the tree and bend the branches so as to bring the tips within reach. Usually the branches break off and, if they don't fall to the ground when the bear is finished with them, they end up lodged in the tree crotch where the bear was sitting. Sometimes really big accumulations of branches (locally called "bear's nests") result and when the leaves are off the trees they are highly conspicuous.

Needless to say, it is a bad day for a Beech tree when a bear pays a visit like this. Not only does it lose much of its beechnut production, but also it gets severely damaged in the process and its eventual death through fungal infection is greatly hastened.

Life is difficult, even for a "timeless" organism like a Beech tree.

Blue Beech

Carpinus caroliniana

Charme de Caroline   Photos page 39

Blue Beech is a small, understory tree that is typically found on rich bottomland soils of southern Ontario and points south. It is not at all the sort of tree one would normally associate with Algonquin. The discovery in 1971 of two Blue Beech stands in feeder valleys of the Petawawa River below Lake Travers was therefore quite unexpected but it did underscore in dramatic fashion the Park's remarkable botanical diversity. The proximity of Black Spruce bogs typical of the far north on the one hand and rich alluvial forests of Blue Beech typical of "down south" is probably duplicated nowhere else.

How our Blue Beech trees actually got here is an interesting question. The best guess is that the Algonquin stands date from a few thousand years ago when a temporary, very warm period in the Earth's history allowed southern tree species like Blue Beech to spread northwards and occupy large, more or less continuous areas north of their present range. Later, when the climate cooled, the southern invaders mostly died out but occasionally survived in isolated pockets where conditions were (and continue to be) especially favourable.

Blue Beech has smooth bark with a rippling "muscled" appearance and its fruit is borne on curious, leaflike structures that probably serve to make the fruit "flutter away" from the vicinity of the parent tree.

Basswood

Tilia americana

Tilleul d'Amérique

White Elm

Ulmus americana

Orme d'Amérique

These species are excellent illustrations of the effect exercised on tree distribution by the higher altitude, and therefore cooler climate, of Algonquin's west side. Elm and Basswood completely surround the Park and both are reasonably common on the east side—Elm on river floodplains and Basswood on open rocky or rich sandy slopes. Basswood is also found scattered through moist deciduous woods in the extreme southern part of the Park.

In the higher elevations of the Algonquin dome (the Park's west side), however, the situation changes radically. Basswood is only rarely found in small groups on rich, south-facing (and therefore warmer) slopes. This is a pity because these trees are very beautiful in their own way, exuding a kind of southern charm. They can be important for wildlife, too, since big trees are usually hollow and afford shelter for Raccoons, Barred Owls, and other creatures.

Elm, too, is quite uncommon at the higher elevations, being found in the very odd pocket of open damp woods or along major valleys such as those of the Nipissing and Madawaska rivers. Even with this isolated distribution, many Elms in Algonquin were infected by the deadly Dutch elm disease that decimated the species in southern Ontario. We have been encouraged in recent years, however, by an apparent comeback of apparently healthy young elm trees and we hope that someday this graceful tree will be restored to its rightful place in Algonquin.

Photos page 39

John Hickie

Summer Beech foliage

Michael Runtz

Beech in fall

Small Beech keep dead leaves

Nancy Checko

Mary I. Moore

Beech leaves turning colour

John Hickie

Bear claw marks

A "bear's nest" in a Beech

Algonquin Park Museum

Harry A. Thomson

Opening Beechnuts

Steve Desjardins

Husks and nuts

A new Beech starting out

John Hickie

25

Pin Cherry
Prunus pensylvanica
Cerisier de Pennsylvanie

Choke Cherry
Prunus virginiana
Cerisier de Virginie

Black Cherry
Prunus serotina
Cerisier tardif

Photos page 29

The Pin Cherry and the Choke Cherry are alike insofar as both are small trees, rarely reaching more than ten metres in height—and usually much smaller—and in their extreme intolerance to shade. Choke Cherry tends to be found in moist sites such as near streams and bogs and Pin Cherry is found in drier, more upland situations, typically in areas that have been ravaged by fires or violent storms.

Pin Cherry especially is a very fast growing tree that quickly colonizes a suitable area and, for a while, may be quite dominant. This is quite temporary, however, because new cherry seedlings cannot grow in the dense shade of their pioneering parents. For the species to survive at all, the seeds must be transported to possibly quite distant, suitable areas, wherever those might be.

The problem faced by Pin Cherries and Choke Cherries, of course, is how to get their seeds to the new areas. Other pioneer tree species, such as the aspens for example, have come up with the solution of producing very tiny, tassel-bearing seeds that can be borne by the wind but cherries accomplish dispersal of their seeds by very different means. Their seeds are enclosed by good-tasting flesh that some birds find very nutritious. Robins and Cedar Waxwings, for example, regularly consume the fruits of Pin and Choke Cherry trees and later regurgitate or defecate the seeds (cherry stones) far from the source trees. Both partners in the relationship gain from the arrangement (the birds get fed and the trees get their seeds dispersed) and the solution might seem to be ideal.

There are problems, however. Black Bears are also attracted by ripe cherries and although the stones pass through the bears unharmed and thus get dispersed almost the same as if a bird had eaten the cherries, the bears sometimes do real damage to the trees. Indeed, in years of good cherry crops, it is common to see whole groves of severely smashed and broken Pin and Choke Cherry trees. Then too, there are other visitors to cherry trees that don't "play by the rules". Chipmunks usually eat only the cherry flesh but sometimes they will take the time to gnaw through the hard outer shell of the cherry stone to eat the big nutritious seed within. Even worse from the trees' point of view, there is one bird, the Evening Grosbeak, that invariably discards the cherry flesh and breaks open the hard cherry stones with its massive, vise-like bill. It is remarkable to stand beside a cherry grove in mid-summer and listen to a flock of Evening Grosbeaks destroying hundreds of cherry stones—each one of which requires a pressure of more than 10 kg to crack. Obviously, the seed dispersal system of our cherries does work some of the time—or else there wouldn't be any Pin and Choke Cherry trees out there. But, as with many systems in nature, it is far from 100% efficient.

Pin Cherry photos opposite, Choke Cherry photos page 29

Most of us think of cherry trees as rather small and something that people cultivate in orchards. This species, however, is a true forest giant which, while scarce, is a natural part of the hardwood stands on Algonquin's west side. Especially since the leaves and flowers are high overhead in the general forest canopy one of the best recognition features of the Black Cherry is the tall trunk and the dark gray bark with distinctive, squarish plates. When the leaves are off the trees another help in identification is provided by the characteristic black swellings in the twigs caused by "Black Knot", a parasitic fungus which attacks this and other species of cherry.

Although the Black Cherry is fairly easy to recognize, you will never see very many of them, let alone encounter a pure stand. As with so many other tree species in Algonquin's west side hardwoods, the presence of a Black Cherry here and there has more to do with luck than anything else. Especially as it gets older, Black Cherry is only moderately tolerant of shade and normally has no chance of out-competing the Sugar Maples that so overwhelmingly dominate well-drained soils on the Park's west side. Only when there is a disturbance such as a violent windstorm that knocks down one or several old trees, combined with the presence of a small cherry seedling in a position to profit from the sudden flood of sunshine, will there be even a possibility of a mature Black Cherry getting established. Even then it helps if the site is more on the moist side so that competing Sugar Maples do less well than they otherwise might.

Along with the very scarce Basswood and Elm, the cherries are the only trees in Algonquin Park that have "perfect" flowers. These are flowers in which both male (pollen-producing) and female (seed-producing) parts are combined into one structure—as opposed to the arrangement in all our other trees which have quite separate male and female flowers. The separate flower arrangement of most trees means that they must rely on wind to blow pollen from the male flowers to the female flowers but the "perfect" arrangement of cherry blossoms opens up another possibility. If insects can be encouraged to visit cherry flowers they have the potential to carry pollen from the male part of one flower and leave it with the female part of the next, thus assuring cross-fertilization. This would seem to be a much more efficient process than producing "tons" of wind-blown pollen, most of which, of course, will land on something other than a female flower. All that has to be done to ensure that insects actually do perform the job of transporting pollen from one flower to the next is to bribe them into visiting flowers (by providing them with sugar-rich nectar) and making sure that the flowers are easy to find. That is why cherry and other insect-pollinated flowers have evolved fragrance and conspicuous petals (white in the case of cherries) that are not needed or possessed by wind-pollinated trees.

John Hickie

Pin Cherries in fall

John Hickie

Pin Cherries in flower

Michael Runtz

Green and red at same time

Michael Runtz

Wrecked by a bear

John Hickie

Leaves in summer

... and fall

John Hickie

Closeup of flowers

John Hickie

Mary I. Moore

Pin Cherry fruit

27

Sugar Maple
Acer saccharum
Érable à sucre

Photos page 31

Many visitors to Algonquin are impressed by all the conifers and imagine they have arrived in "the north woods". This is true up to a point but the fact remains that most of the Park, particularly the west side, is largely covered by forests of deciduous, broad-leaved hardwood trees. Of these, by far the most common is the Sugar Maple, a tree which quickly drops out of the forest as you go north from Algonquin but which is very much part of the scene in almost every southern Ontario woodlot and even as far south as Tennessee. Many people, if not already familiar with this decidedly southern species from trees growing in their yards back home, know the Sugar Maple as the source of maple syrup and the tree whose leaf appears on the Canadian flag.

Here in Algonquin, it is the tree most responsible for the Park's famous fall colours, it is a cornerstone of Algonquin's thirty-five million dollar a year logging industry, and it has an overwhelming ecological importance. Although, in a way, it has rather narrow requirements—moist, well-drained hills covered with glacial till—there is so much of this land type on the Park's west side that Sugar Maple covers vast areas and in those areas it is the undisputed king. Sixty to seventy percent of the trees in typical west side hardwood forests are Sugar Maple and, with time, this percentage often tends to increase.

Sugar Maples produce enormous quantities of large, winged seeds (often as many as half a million per hectare even in a bad year and perhaps over ten million in a good one) and the resulting seedlings are superbly adapted to the conditions prevailing in maple forests. They are so large and vigorous that, unlike the tiny seedlings of most other trees, their emerging roots can penetrate the thick layer of dead leaves on the forest floor and get established in the soil below. Sugar Maple seeds can even germinate under the snow in early spring, thereby gaining a one to two month jump over competing species. Most other trees don't stand a chance unless their seeds happen to land on an old rotting log or where the matted maple leaves have been removed by fire or some other disturbance. Even then there is no guarantee of victory against the Sugar Maple. The forest floor in maple stands is covered with hundreds of thousands of maple seedlings. Although their growth has been stalled at about a metre high or less by the dense shade of the parent trees overhead, the seedlings can live on for several years and respond quickly if the death of an old tree should improve light conditions. Very often, in fact, Sugar Maple seedlings are the only contestants present when a race opens up to fill a gap left in the forest canopy and, even when there is competition, conditions have to be quite special for Sugar Maple to lose out.

Quite obviously, Sugar Maple has a tremendous control over the destinies of its own seedlings and those of other trees, but the influence goes far beyond this. For example, the summer shade of a maple forest is so complete that life is next to impossible for small plants down on the forest floor. There is a brief period, however, between the melting of the last snow around the beginning of May and the leafing out of the trees when the forest floor is exposed to bright sunlight. This is the one, narrow window available to small flowering plants in the hardwood forests and several species including trilliums, Spring Beauties, and Trout Lilies have adapted their yearly cycles to take advantage of it. They spring up, flower, and in some cases entirely disappear, leaves and all, when the maples plunge the forest back into shade.

Another far-reaching influence of the Sugar Maple is exerted through seed production. Maple seeds are the principal food of Algonquin's most common mammal, the Deer Mouse, but because seed production goes up and down so wildly from one year to the next, the mouse population follows suit. And, since so many larger animals, from owls, to foxes, to weasels, depend on the mice, the weather-induced fluctuations of Sugar Maple seed production send major ecological ripples out through the Park's wildlife community.

Clearly the Sugar Maple is a major player in Algonquin in more ways than one.

Red Maple
Acer rubrum
Érable rouge

Photos page 30

Red Maple may fairly be called a plastic, opportunistic tree. It can, and frequently does, grow in hardwood stands with Sugar Maple and there attains the size and proportions of normal forest trees. It also and perhaps more typically grows, however, in places that Sugar Maple can't inhabit—dry, rocky hillsides or wet, mucky soil beside bogs and beaver ponds. In these sites Red Maple tends to be a much smaller, sprawling sort of a tree, frequently with multiple trunks.

Because it often takes root in partly disturbed fringe areas before other trees move in and eventually replace it, Red Maple is sometimes considered to be a pioneer species. In keeping with this idea, Red Maple has very light seed, capable of long dispersal distances (with luck to new, temporarily suitable sites). It also flowers very early in the spring and releases its seed in late June long before other trees, and possibly giving Red Maple an advantage in the competition for new sites.

In the summer, Red Maple may easily be told from Sugar Maple by the sharp notches between the leaf lobes (not rounded or U-shaped as in Sugar Maple). At other times of the year its identity is revealed by the bright red colour somewhere in its anatomy—red twigs in winter, red buds and flowers in spring, and brilliant red leaves in fall.

The maples are famous as the Park's most flamboyantly coloured trees in the fall (with the peak coming usually in the last week of September or sometimes the first week of October). Sugar Maple leaves may turn red or orange but often—especially below the canopy—they are quite yellow. With Red Maple, however, the colour of an individual tree's fall foliage depends more on the tree's sex than anything else. Unlike Sugar Maples which always bear both male and female flowers on the same tree, Red Maples have segregated sexes. There are male trees (with nothing but male flowers) and there are female trees with only female flowers. In the fall, male Red Maples go various shades of red, ranging from vermillion to scarlet and light to dark, whereas the leaves on female Red Maples change to different tones of yellow to orange.

We humans find these colour changes breathtaking but we usually assume that they are just accidental by-products of death in the leaves. In fact, they are outward signs of an important chemical salvage operation.

Leaves are green in summer because they contain chlorophyll, the amazing chemical that captures much of the sun's energy which is then used to combine water and carbon dioxide to make sugars and, from them, starch, cellulose, and all the other complex substances that make up a tree. But, in addition to the chemicals they themselves have manufactured, leaves also contain minute but precious quantities of simpler substances originally obtained through the tree's roots from the soil. These substances, often called "minerals" or "nutrients", include magnesium (an essential component of chlorophyll), nitrogen (part of all proteins), and others such as calcium, phosphorus, and potassium. Most of a tree's nutrients are contained in its leaves and it would not be very efficient to lose them all when the leaves are shed in the fall. In fact, most trees start removing nitrogen and other nutrients from their leaves almost as soon as the long, prime growing days of June and early July are over. This continues until the leaf finally loses its ability to manufacture chlorophyll, the existing chlorophyll breaks down, and yellow pigments that were there all along are exposed for the first time. By this time, half of the leaf's nutrients have been removed back into the tree (for use in manufacturing next year's leaves) but many nutrients still remain out in the leaves. It is at this point that maples manufacture their red pigments (called anthocyanins) from excess sugars, and there is some evidence that they protect the leaves from cold and ultraviolet light. If so, they probably serve to prolong the life of the leaves for a few extra days and permit the nutrient "bucket brigade" to operate that much longer.

Michael Runtz

Black Cherry in fall colours

Dan Strickland

Black Cherries are forest giants

John Hickie

Black Cherry flowers

Black Cherry fruit

John Hickie

Black knot fungus is common on cherries

John Hickie

Michael Runtz

Choke Cherry in fall

John Hickie

Choke Cherry flowers

Ontario Tree Seed Plant

Choke Cherry fruit

John Hickie

Male Red Maples turn red

And female Red Maples turn yellow!

Michael Runtz

John Hickie

Red (left) and Sugar Maple leaves

John Hickie

Moose love bark

William Reynolds

Note V-shaped notches of Red Maple

John Hickie

Female flowers of Red Maple

Mary I. Moore

Male flowers of Red Maple early in spring

Harry A. Thomson

Red Maple keys

Algonquin Park Museum

John Hickie

The dominance of Sugar Maple is revealed in fall

Sugar Maple foliage in fall

Dan Strickland

Crowns touch to form forest canopy

John Hickie

Carpet of Sugar Maple seedlings

John Hickie

Looking up at the crown of a Sugar Maple

Michael Runtz

Bisexual flowers appear with leaves

Mary I. Moore

Sugar Maple keys

John Hickie

Humble beginnings of a Sugar Maple

31

Silver Maple

Acer saccharinum

Érable argenté

Silver Maple is a rare tree in Algonquin and not likely to be seen here by most visitors. Nevertheless, the way its distribution is restricted in the Park raises some interesting points. It is familiar to many people as a planted ornamental in city streets and parks but its natural habitat is in swamps or rich, periodically inundated floodplains along rivers. As such it is a common sight in southern Ontario but hardly to be expected on the Precambrian Shield generally, much less in the Algonquin uplands. It can be seen, however, in one rich alluvial pocket along the Oxtongue River on the Park's west side and in several places along the Bonnechère, Barron, and Petawawa rivers on the east side. Whitson Lake on the Petawawa has particularly large Silver Maple forests on several silty islands.

The whole question of Silver Maple in Algonquin could use some serious study, however, because even if some true Silver Maple trees are present here, many more trees are evidently hybrids between Silver Maple and Red Maple. These so-called "United" maples or "Pink" maples show a bewildering gradation from pure Silver to pure Red and very little is known of their distribution or genetics.

Mountain Maple

Acer spicatum

Érable à épis

Like the following species Mountain Maple is very small, often more of a shrub than a tree but it is undeniably a maple and we have chosen to include it in this book. Here in Algonquin, Mountain Maple is nearing the southern edge of its range for it is primarily a tree of northern boreal forests where it grows on richer sites in association with Trembling Aspen, Balsam Fir, and White Spruce. Under these trees, with their rather open canopies, enough light is admitted to maintain an understory of Mountain Maples, and their gorgeous orange foliage is an attractive feature of the true north woods each fall. In the hardwood forests of Sugar Maple and Yellow Birch which occupy Algonquin, the forest canopy normally has a "closed" structure which blocks off so much light that Mountain Maple cannot survive. Only in special situations such as steep-sided valleys is enough light admitted, "from the side" as it were, to permit Mountain Maple to establish and maintain a toehold in the Park.

Striped Maple

Acer pensylvanicum

Érable de Pennsylvanie

Striped Maple is a very small tree, only rarely reaching 10 metres in height and 15 cm in trunk diameter, but it often attracts notice with its enormous, three-pointed leaves and striking, bright green, vertically striped bark. It is a characteristic associate of Algonquin's west side hardwood and Hemlock forests and appears whenever a temporary sun-lit clearing is opened up among the mature trees. At first, its crown rises in the sun but, eventually, a Striped Maple's fate is to be overtopped by surrounding Sugar Maples or other larger trees. With the return of shady conditions, Striped Maples die out, only to reappear elsewhere when wind, old age, or some other agent punches a new hole in the forest canopy.

Black Ash

Fraxinus nigra

Frêne noir Photos page 37

This species is the only one of the Park's three ashes that could be called common and even it is restricted to widely scattered, swampy pockets or "swales" where the soil is nutrient rich and occasionally saturated with standing, shallow water in the spring and early summer. In these situations it often grows in pure stands, however, indicating that it is well adapted to such specialized conditions. Any doubt about the identity of Black Ash can be removed by touching the bark. It is light gray and surprisingly soft and "corky" to the touch. The ashes are the only trees in Algonquin that have compound leaves, that is leaves composed of several separate leaflets. In the case of Black Ash, there are from 7 to 11 leaflets in each leaf and each is connected directly to the main leaf stalk.

Most trees have evolved some mechanism for dispersing their seeds away from the parent tree so as to maximize the chances that at least some will end up in a favourable location. The poplars have tiny seeds that are borne aloft by long white hairs attached at one end, and the cherries enclose their seeds in an edible fruit that is carried away by birds or bears. The mechanism employed by the majority of Algonquin trees, however, is the provision of stiff, bladelike "seed wings" that stick out from the sides of the seeds and help retard their fall. The seeds of some trees, notably the birches and the alders have two seed wings, one on each side, but the more usual arrangement is to have just one. All of our tiny conifer seeds have this system and so do the much larger and more familiar maples. The effect, of course, is to make the single-winged seed into a spinning, natural "helicopter" that has an obviously slow rate of fall—and therefore a much greater chance of travelling far from the parent tree before hitting the ground.

The large seeds of ash also have a single seed wing system but one that operates somewhat differently from, and somewhat less efficiently than, that of maples. Lacking the thickened leading edge of maple keys, falling ash seeds not only spin like helicopter blades but also they "roll" on their long axis as they go. This system is aerodynamically less efficient and results in a faster rate of fall and shorter air time than in maples. Nevertheless, given the distinctly localized site requirements for Black Ash, it may be "safer", for the seeds of this species at least, not to stray too far from the neighbourhood of the mother tree.

White Ash

Fraxinus americana

Frêne d'Amérique

Red Ash

Fraxinus pennsylvanica

Frêne de Pennsylvanie

Neither of these species of ash is important in the forests of Algonquin but both occur here. White Ash is an upland tree that just barely makes it into the extreme south and east of the Park. Red Ash, or more specifically a variety that, confusingly, is called Green Ash, is a sprawling river's edge tree that is locally common on the lower Petawawa from Cedar Lake down to the Park boundary at McManus Lake.

Photos page 37

Silver Maples at Whitson Lake

Silver (left) and Red Maple leaves

Leaf of a Red-Silver hybrid

Mountain Maple flowers

Mountain Maple leaves

Striped Maple bark

Striped Maple flowers

Large and distinctive leaves

Striped Maple in fall

Ironwood (Hop Hornbeam)
Ostrya virginiana
Ostryer de Virginie

Ironwood (named for its extreme dense, hard wood) is not a spectacular tree but it is quite common in the forests of the Park's west side. It seldom exceeds the 8-12 metre range in height or 15-25 cm in diameter and therefore achieves its modest success more through opportunism rather than by dominating its neighbours. It rises in shafts of sun that penetrate breaks in the forest canopy and for a while competes well with other trees growing around it. Ironwood survival is best on fresh or moist glacial till with Red Maple, White Birch, Balsam Fir, and White Spruce but in west side hardwoods it is typically overtopped by Sugar Maple or Beech. When this happens the Ironwood is left behind and gradually dies. The death of trees in any forest is an everyday event but the fact that such a small species as Ironwood manages to compete as well and survive as long as it does in the face of competition from much bigger trees is quite remarkable. One has to marvel at the efficiency of Ironwood leaves in converting meagre amounts of solar energy into sugars and other chemical compounds necessary for the tree's growth and maintenance.

The seeds, or nuts, of Ironwood develop in individual, inflated bladders about 2 cm long. This probably keeps the nuts airborne a bit longer when they are shed in winter and increases the area over which they will be dispersed—and therefore the chances of one or two of them landing in a favourable spot for growth.

The bladders also become covered, at the time of nut ripening, by a fine downy coating that is distinctly irritating to the touch. Presumably this helps to deter chipmunks and other seed predators.

Logging in Algonquin Park

No book on the trees of Algonquin would be complete without an account of logging within the Park. From almost every point of view—historical, cultural, economic, ecological, and social—the subject is extremely important. At times, it has also been a very controversial one, with strong emotions expressed on both sides. In this regard, it is not our purpose here to say—as we are so often asked—whether logging in Algonquin is a "good" or "bad" thing. As a matter of fact, the legitimacy of both viewpoints was recognized in the Ontario Government's 1974 Master Plan for Algonquin and that is why logging is permitted in some parts of the Park but not in other zones. It is our intention, however, to describe briefly the history and nature of logging and forest management in Algonquin so that readers may have as accurate a picture of the subject as possible. Too often in the past, people have started out with faulty assumptions about logging in Algonquin—and arguments based on incorrect premises are seldom helpful.

One example of this is the widespread idea that logging in the Park is a new development and represents an erosion of Algonquin's original purpose. In fact, when the Park was established (on about half its present size) back in 1893, logging had already been going on for over 50 years. A map drawn in 1837 identified "logging shanties" on the shore of Lake Travers in what is now the east side of Algonquin. We do not know how much sooner than that the first loggers reached the Park area or how extensive their activities were by then, but we do know at least that, only a few decades later, logging in the Park area was big business indeed. Dr Grant Head of Wilfrid Laurier University has painstakingly sifted through archival records of timber licences, statements of harvest and timber rafts going down the Ottawa River in the last century and pinpointed the origins and volumes of the wood to the point where he has been able to draw maps like the one presented here. This work reveals some rather astonishing levels of activity and a rapid advance into the virgin wilderness of what only much later became Algonquin Park. In the winter of 1866-67, for example, some 30,000 pieces of square timber (White and Red Pine trunks squared by axe to fit into the holds of trans-Atlantic timber ships) were cut here over the winter months by about 600 men, living in primitive, lice-infested hovels cut off from the outside world in a snowy, roadless wilderness. Just twelve winters later, and still 14 years before Algonquin became a Park, almost all the present Park area was under timber licence and over 73,000 sawlogs and 15,000 pieces of square timber were driven down swollen rivers in the spring of 1879 from the Algonquin highlands.

There was no intention then, in 1893 when the Park was proclaimed, to "preserve" an untouched wilderness or even to keep what was left by excluding loggers. The real concerns among Park advocates of the day were the protection of wildlife and halting the advance of subsistence farming which would have cleared away the forests that regulated the flow in over half a dozen major rivers originating in the Algonquin highlands. Indeed, the Park idea, as it was then popularly conceived, was viewed as entirely beneficial to the interests of logging companies and one of them even petitioned the government to extend the Park boundaries so as to include its licence area.

It was only many years later, with the general increase of Park visitors, that a conflict began to develop between the new, recreational and the traditional, "industrial" uses of Algonquin. The management solution to this clash devised by Superintendent Frank MacDougall back in the 1930s was to separate the loggers and recreationists as much as possible by establishing no-logging reservations around shorelines. This basic approach has remained at the core of Algonquin Park's management up to the present although details have changed because of evolving technology. The days of cross-cut saws, horses, and river drives are gone now and logging is presently done with chainsaws, mechanical skidders, and trucks. To maintain the separation of logging and recreation it has therefore been necessary to impose further restrictions on the location of roads, hauling times, and noise levels of equipment.

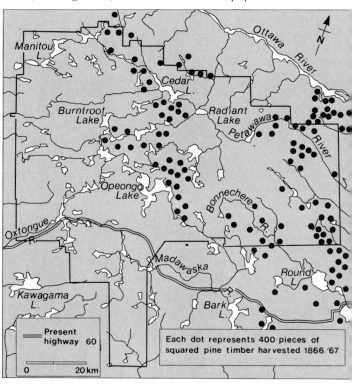

The cutting of pine for square timber in the Algonquin Park area, winter of 1866-67 (Map prepared by Dept. of Geography, Wilfrid Laurier University)

Further changes came too with the Park Master Plan in 1974. That is when the present zoning system was established restricting logging to about 75% of the Park area but away from designated wilderness zones, recreation zones, and environmentally or historically significant sites as well. The Plan also brought about the cancellation of all the existing private timber licences within the Park and the creation of a single Crown Corporation, the Algonquin Forestry Authority, an "umbrella" logging company which now supplies wood to the 20 private logging companies that used to cut in the Park. Since 1983, the Algonquin Forestry Authority (AFA) has also assumed responsibility for managing the Park forests with the Ministry of Natural Resources (which used to do the management) taking on the role of monitoring the AFA's work.

The whole subject of "forest management" is one that is quite foreign to most people and a second area where misconceptions are rife. For one thing, a modern forester manages his forests for much more than just the production of wood. Even in the Park zones where such activity is permitted, the forester sees to it that

Ironwoods are modest hardwoods

Bark and leaves

Ironwood fruit

Michael Runtz

Algonquin Park Museum

Mary I. Moore

Uniform shelterwood cut in White Pine

Last log drive on Petawawa, 1959

Alan G. Gordon

Alan G. Gordon

Ten years after shelterwood cut

Modern slasher operation, east side

Jack Mihell

Marc Denis

Four years after hardwood selection cut

Nowadays logs are trucked out of the Park

Jack Mihell

Algonquin Park Museum

hollow trees are retained for cavity nesting birds and mammals and that conifers and mast (seed) producing trees are kept for other wildlife. Another popular misconception is that "logging" means clear-cutting, after which not a single tree remains standing. In some parts of the world where foresters are managing for the production of trees whose growth requires full sunlight, a clear-cutting system is, in fact, the best approach. Here in Algonquin, however, most of our commercially valuable trees are not managed that way. Instead, cutting systems are used which deliberately leave standing large trees on the logged area at all times. Just how this works can be best seen by looking at how we manage for the Park's two most important commercial species, the Sugar Maple and the White Pine.

The Selection System in Sugar Maple

The aim of a forester working with any tree species is to coax nature to grow the greatest volume of high quality wood in the shortest amount of time but, to do that, he or she must choose an approach to fit the characteristics of the tree in question. In the case of Sugar Maple, we know that young trees are highly tolerant of shade and grow up underneath larger ones, resulting in a forest containing trees of many different ages and sizes. A clear-cut would not make sense in such a situation for two reasons. First, it would result in the cutting of many small, not yet useful, trees along with the big ones. Second, it would create treeless, sunny conditions in which some other less valuable tree species would do better than Sugar Maple and take over the site. If the forest is going to continue producing Sugar Maple, therefore, the forester must use some sort of "selection" system in which only some of the bigger trees are removed at any one time. The trick is doing this so as to maximize the stand's long term production. This is one of those things that is easier said than done and it took a great deal of careful work at the Park's Forest Research Station, located at Swan Lake, to clarify the problem. Everyone knows that sunlight is required for trees to put on growth, and other things being equal, a single, sunbathed Sugar Maple tree standing alone on a hectare patch of land would grow very well indeed. The problem, from the forester's point of view, would be that there would still only be one tree on that hectare and, no matter how well the tree grew, the hectare would not be producing very much wood. At the other extreme, the hectare might have several thousand trees but all crowded in so close together that none of them would receive enough sunlight to do more than grow very slowly. In fact, the net wood production in such a situation might well be zero because the growth of new wood on the hectare could be balanced by the loss of unhealthy, marginal trees to disease.

Somewhere between these two extremes of one tree and too many trees, however, there is a happy medium where the hectare has a good number of trees but spaced widely enough apart that each one of them gets enough sunlight to put on rapid growth. In Algonquin Park this happy medium is reached when the total cross-sectional area of Sugar Maple tree trunks greater than 25 cm in diameter is 12.3 square metres per hectare of forest (60 square feet per acre). A stand that is stocked at this level will, in a mere 20 years, grow from 12.3 square metres of tree trunk area per hectare to 20 square metres, representing an approximate doubling of the volume of Sugar Maple wood. After the 20 years are up the growth is slowing down but it is at this point that loggers come in and cut pre-selected, marked trees representing 7.7 square metres of Sugar Maple tree trunk per hectare. This, of course, once again leaves 12.3 square metres per hectare—the "magic level" leading to the greatest possible growth of Sugar Maple over the next 20 years and so on down the line.

The advantages of such a system are several—production is maximized, the forest always remains in Sugar Maple and the aesthetics are much more pleasing than with a clear-cut. It is also possible, by deliberately selecting and marking the poorer quality trees for removal and leaving the best ones, to upgrade the quality of the forest. Before the adoption of the present selection system in the 1970s the quality of Algonquin's hardwood forests had actually been decreasing because logging companies quite naturally tended to take the best trees and leave the poorer ones. Now, and for the rest of this century, most of the cutting will be directed towards low value trees and the quality of the remaining forest will therefore be upgraded. After that, subsequent cutting cycles should enjoy the best of two worlds; they will harvest the maximum sustained volume the land is capable of producing and also the maximum sustained quality.

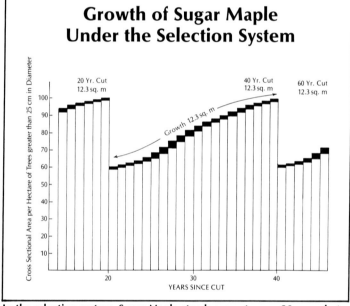

Basal Area of Sugar Maple Trees

Growth of Sugar Maple is maximized when trees are spaced so that total cross-sectional area at breast height of trees greater than 25 cm in diameter (sum of shaded areas) is equal to 12.3 square metres per hectare of forest (60 square feet per acre).

Growth of Sugar Maple Under the Selection System

20 Yr. Cut 12.3 sq. m

40 Yr. Cut 12.3 sq. m

60 Yr. Cut 12.3 sq. m

Growth 12.3 sq. m

Cross Sectional Area per Hectare of Trees greater than 25 cm in Diameter

YEARS SINCE CUT

In the selection system, Sugar Maple stands are cut every 20 years but always leaving the density of trees (12.3 square metres per hectare of trunk cross-sectional area) where growth will be at a maximum. In this way the land always remains forested and the volume of wood approximately doubles before the next cut.

Uniform Shelterwood in White Pine

The White Pine stands on Algonquin's east side are by far the most significant remaining source in Ontario for this valuable wood, and it is very important that they be managed to continue that way. However, making sure that cut White Pine trees are succeeded by new ones is considerably more difficult than with Sugar Maple.

Trees in a White Pine stand are often the same age—suggesting that all of them could be cut at the same time in a single clear-cut. But although young White Pines need more sunlight than maple seedlings, the full light created by a clear-cut can be just as damaging as too much shade, chiefly by promoting the growth of more vigorous sun-loving shrubs or trees that outcompete young pines. Anything more than 40-50% direct sunlight will also encourage the attacks of an insect, the White Pine Weevil, which destroys the young tree's leader (uppermost part of the stem) and results in lower quality wood (due to the persisting crook in the trunk). As before, the trick is to find the happy medium to allow in just the right amount of sunlight. At one time, the pine forests of Algonquin were managed using a "strip-cut" system in which parallel, north-south strips of forest, 66 to

John Hickie

Black Ash foliage turns yellow

Michael Runtz

Riverside Red Ash

Alan G. Gordon

Black Ash

Michael Runtz

Black Ash bark

Michael Runtz

One Black Ash leaf (9 leaflets)

Ontario Tree Seed Plant

White Ash seeds

Harry A. Thomson

Ash flowers

37

100 feet wide, were cleared of all trees while leaving intervening strips of forest untouched. The idea was that sun would penetrate into the cleared strips but the trees in the adjacent uncut strips would provide the needed seed and the right amount of shade.

This method had indifferent success, however, so another system, called "uniform shelterwood" was adopted in 1975. In this approach, a mature pine stand is removed in a series of four cuts at 20 year intervals. Although these cuts thin out the stand more and more, the crowns of remaining trees expand after each cut and tend to keep the sunlight on the forest floor below in the desirable 40-50% range. This makes for maximum growth while guarding against White Pine Weevil problems. By the time of the fourth cut, when the last of the overhead trees are removed, 60 years have elapsed since the first cut and the new, even-aged stand of pine that was established in the shelter of the old trees is now ready to stand on its own and grow for another forty years before the cycle starts over again.

The fundamental point, whether we are dealing with the selection system in hardwoods, the uniform shelterwood system in pines or some other system involving a different tree species, is that logging in Algonquin is just one part—albeit the payoff part—in a "management cycle". Cutting is not done merely to take what is there and without any concern for what follows. Instead, it is done in carefully researched ways that seek to maximize the land's production of desired tree species and to continue that production, cycle after cycle, on into the future. Moreover, the management systems used in Algonquin Park almost always mean that trees remain standing on the land at all times and many people would be hard pressed to realize that logging had even taken place in most areas just a few years later.

Uniform Shelterwood Management of White Pine

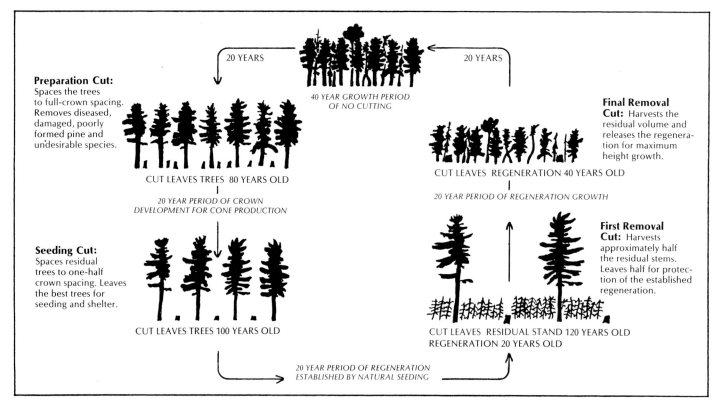

Preparation Cut: Spaces the trees to full-crown spacing. Removes diseased, damaged, poorly formed pine and undesirable species.

20 YEARS

40 YEAR GROWTH PERIOD OF NO CUTTING

20 YEARS

Final Removal Cut: Harvests the residual volume and releases the regeneration for maximum height growth.

CUT LEAVES TREES 80 YEARS OLD

20 YEAR PERIOD OF CROWN DEVELOPMENT FOR CONE PRODUCTION

CUT LEAVES REGENERATION 40 YEARS OLD

20 YEAR PERIOD OF REGENERATION GROWTH

Seeding Cut: Spaces residual trees to one-half crown spacing. Leaves the best trees for seeding and shelter.

First Removal Cut: Harvests approximately half the residual stems. Leaves half for protection of the established regeneration.

CUT LEAVES TREES 100 YEARS OLD

CUT LEAVES RESIDUAL STAND 120 YEARS OLD REGENERATION 20 YEARS OLD

20 YEAR PERIOD OF REGENERATION ESTABLISHED BY NATURAL SEEDING

Introduced Trees in Algonquin Park

The following tree species have been deliberately or inadvertently planted in Algonquin Park. Although they are of negligible importance in the Park as a whole, they are usually found in places frequented by Park visitors and tend to be seen rather often. This is particularly true with the rather extensive stands of Scot's Pine at Pog, Kearney, and Rock Lake campgrounds.

Norway Spruce	*Picea abies*
Serbian Spruce	*Picea omorika*
Mugho Pine	*Pinus mugo*
Scot's Pine	*Pinus sylvestris*
Whitebark Pine	*Pinus albicaulis*
Silver Poplar	*Populus alba*
Gray Poplar	*Populus canescens*
Lombardy Poplar	*Populus nigra*
Amur Maple	*Acer ginnala*
Manitoba Maple	*Acer negundo*

For Further Information

We hope you have enjoyed this book on the trees of Algonquin Park and would be happy to answer any further questions you may have; please address them to:

Park Superintendent
Algonquin Provincial Park
Box 219
Whitney, Ontario
K0J 2M0

You may also wish to consult the following selected references:

1. *Native Trees of Canada* (tree identification) by R.C. Hosie, 1967, Seventh edition, Canadian Forestry Service, Ottawa.
2. *Sylvics of Forest Trees of the United States*, Agriculture Handbook No. 271, Forest Service, U.S.D.A.
3. *Management of Tolerant Hardwoods in Algonquin Provincial Park*, 1983, Forest Management Branch, Division of Forests, Ontario Ministry of Natural Resources.
4. *A Silvicultural Guide to the White Pine Working Group*, 1973, Ontario Ministry of Natural Resources.
5. *Forest Management Plan, Algonquin Provincial Park* (for the period 1990-2010), 1990, Algonquin Forestry Authority, Huntsville, Ontario.
6. *Nineteenth Century Timbering and Sawlogging in the Ottawa Valley: Documentary Sources and Spatial Patterns*, 1980, by C. Grant Head in: *Exploring Our Heritage: The Ottawa Valley Experience*, Ontario Ministry of Culture and Recreation.

Harry A. Thomson

American Elm in spring

William J. Crins

Blue Beech trunks are "muscled"

Elm leaves

Michael Runtz

Blue Beech leaves

Michael Runtz

Basswood

Michael Runtz

Basswood flowers

Michael Runtz

... and fruit

Annotated Checklist of the Indigenous Trees of Algonquin Park

The following annotated list includes thirty-four tree species native to Algonquin Park and selected additional information. Under "Status" there is an indication of whether the species is common (C), uncommon (U), or rare (R), and a second symbol indicates that the species is largely or entirely restricted to either the west side (W) or east side (E) of the Park.

Under "Uses of Wood" are listed the chief and (secondary) commercial uses to which wood cut in Algonquin Park is put. The column "Annual Volume Cut" gives the average volume of wood cut by species for the period 1986-1995.

Tree	Status	Principal and (Secondary) Commercial Uses of Wood Cut in Park	Average Annual Volume Cut (1986-1995) in Cubic Metres
Pine Family			
Balsam Fir	C	Construction lumber, (fine paper pulp, e.g., for photographic print paper)	3,698
Tamarack	C	— — —	— —
White Spruce	C		
Red Spruce	UW	Construction lumber, (fine paper pulp, e.g., for photographic print paper)	18,108
Black Spruce	C		
Jack Pine	CE	Construction lumber	1,234
Red Pine	C	Telephone poles, construction lumber, furniture	30,838
White Pine	C	Mouldings, pattern stock, solid panelling	61,724
White Cedar	C	(Shingles)—cedar only cut in Park from road rights-of-way	16
Eastern Hemlock	C	Construction lumber, (fine paper pulp, e.g., for photographic print paper)	20,986
Willow Family			
Balsam Poplar	U	Construction lumber, (specialty lumber products)	
Largetooth Aspen	C	Construction lumber, fine paper pulp, specialty lumber products,	58,572
Trembling Aspen	C	matches, landscaping squares, chipboard	
Hazel Family			
Speckled Alder	C	— —	— —
Yellow Birch	C	Construction lumber, furniture, veneer panelling, pallets, fine paper pulp,	15,144
White Birch	C	railway ties, firewood	19,424
Blue Beech	RE	— —	— —
Ironwood	C	— —	
Beech Family			
American Beech	C	Construction lumber, furniture, pallets, fine paper pulp, railroad ties, tool handles, firewood	25,907
Bur Oak	RE	— —	— —
Red Oak	C	Furniture, veneer and solid panelling, railroad ties, flooring, specialty lumber products, (firewood)	552
Elm Family			
American Elm	U	— —	— .
Rose Family			
Pin Cherry	C	— —	— –
Black Cherry	UW	Furniture, veneer and solid panelling, canoe paddles, (firewood)	716
Choke Cherry	C	— —	— —
Maple Family			
Striped Maple	C	— —	— —
Silver Maple	UE	— —	— —
Red Maple	C	Construction lumber, furniture, pallets, fine paper pulp, railroad ties,	121,345
Sugar Maple	C	flooring, canoe paddles, specialty lumber products, firewood	
Mountain Maple	C	— —	— —
Linden Family			
Basswood	U	Furniture, specialty lumber products, mouldings, cupboards, (solid panelling)	1,191
Olive Family			
White Ash	R	Veneer panelling, snowshoe frames, (pallets, railway ties)	160
Black Ash	C	— —	— —
Red (Green) Ash	UE	— —	— —

Economic Significance			
Volume Cut		Total of Above Average Annual Volumes (1986-1995)	379,615
Revenue		Annual Stumpage Revenue to Ontario (1986-1995)	$1,256,703
		Annual Value Added by Logging and Manufacturing	$70,988,000 (approx.)
		Provincial and Federal Tax Revenues	$20,303,000 (approx.)
Annual Employment Person-years		Ministry of Natural Resources	7
		Algonquin Forestry Authority	45
		Logging	355
		Primary Manufacturing	1,800
		Total of Above	2, 207